INTRODUCTION _____

Tips on pronunciation
and phonetics

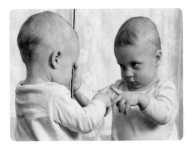

Langenscheidt Wortschatz

Deutsch als Fremdsprache
Bild für Bild

Langenscheidt
München · Wien

Herausgegeben von der Langenscheidt-Redaktion

Idee: Langenscheidt-Redaktion
Kreative Umsetzung und Autoren Beispielsätze:
Arndt Knieper, Martin Waller
Projektleitung und Redaktion: Martin Waller
Design und Layout: Arndt Knieper
Englische Übersetzung: Helen Galloway
Gesamtproduktion: Werkstatt München – Buchproduktion
Covergestaltung: Fuchs Design, München

www.langenscheidt.de

© 2017 Langenscheidt GmbH & Co. KG
Satz: Anja Dengler, Werkstatt München
Druck und Bindung: Druckerei C. H. Beck, Nördlingen

ISBN 978-3-468-20224-7

17010

Do you find studying boring? Fancy having fun while you learn?

Then Langenscheidt's Bild für Bild is the vocabulary trainer for you. Its completely new approach guarantees a highly enjoyable and successful learning experience.

So how does it work? It is well known that associating a word with a memorable picture and using the word in an example sentence helps you to memorize it. Well, this method works even better if it makes you laugh. Your memory is much likelier to retain a humorous or ironic association between the word, picture and example sentence. This means that you can have fun and still learn a lot at the same time.

die **Zahnbürste**
['tsaːnbʏrstə] *n*
the toothbrush

Die Zahnbürste war ein sicheres
Zeichen: Sie würde bleiben.
*The toothbrush was a sure sign
that she would stay.*

der **Föhn**
[føːn] *n*
the hairdryer

Dass ein einfacher Föhn solche
Gefühle wecken kann ...
*You wouldn't think that a
humble hairdryer could awaken
such feelings ...*

die **Haarbürste**
['haːebʏrstə] *n*
the hairbrush

die **Seife**
['zaɪfə] *n*
the soap

die **Creme**
[kreːm] *n*
the cream

die **Zahnpasta**
['tsaːnpasta] *n*
the toothpaste

1 The vocabulary is divided into five major areas of our lives. The words have been selected based on their frequency, topicality and usefulness. Grouping them together by theme makes them even easier to learn.

2 Additional word lists supplement and expand the vocabulary.

3 arbeiten
['aʁbaɪtən] *v*
to work

4 Bis zu den Knien im Dreck:
Das nenn' ich arbeiten!
*Up to my knees in muck:
that's what I call working!*

3 For every word, we also show its part of speech, its pronunciation using the International Phonetic Alphabet (see page 8) and its German translation.

4 In addition, different colours are used for the different parts of speech:

Nouns = blue
Verbs = red
Adjectives and
adverbs = green
Function words = purple
Phrases = black

haben
[ˈhaːbən] *v*
to have (got)

Seit heute habe ich einen
richtig guten Freund.
*From now on I've got a
really good friend.*

Haben is also an auxiliary verb to indicate the present perfect of many verbs: *Ich habe neue Teller gekauft –* "I have bought some new plates."
A synonym of *haben* as a full verb is *besitzen* (to possess).

5

5 "Post-it notes" contain tips on usage and how to tell the difference between words that are easily confused, as well as other aspects of the language such as word formation.

And if you are searching for a specific word, you can find it in one of the separate indexes for each language at the back of the book.

ABBREVIATIONS:

adj	adjective
adv	adverb
conj	conjunction
etw.	etwas
f	feminine
interj	interjection
m	masculine
m/f	masculine and feminine
n	noun
phrase	phrase
pl	plural
prep	preposition
pron	pronoun
sg	singular
sth.	something
v	verb

Vowels

SYMBOL	EXAMPLE	PRONUNCIATION
[a]	gef a llen	similar to **a** in British English c **a** t
[a:]	B a hn, ein p aa r	like **a** in f **a** ther
[ɛ]	am b e sten, e ssen	like **e** in b **e** d
[e:]	l e sen, s e hr, T ee	formed similarly to a long [i:] but with the mouth a bit more open
[ə]	bitt e , dank e	non-stressed -e endings, like **a** in **a** bout
[ɪ]	du b i st, r i cht i g	like **i** in l **i** st
[i:]	Kant i ne, L ie be	like **ee** in s **ee**
[ɔ]	o ffen, P o st	similar to **o** in n **o** t
[o:]	O bst, w o hnen	formed similarly to [ɔ] but with the lips more rounded and closed
[ʊ]	u m, L u st	like **u** in p **u** t
[u:]	U hr, Radt ou r, J u ni	like **ou** in y **ou**

Diphthongs and umlauts

SYMBOL	EXAMPLE	PRONUNCIATION
[aɪ]	M ai , h ei ßen (Bayer, Meyer)	like **y** in m **y**
[au]	Au to, eink au fen	like **ou** in m **ou** th
[ɔʏ]	R äu me, n eu , t eu er	like **oy** in b **oy**
[ɛ]	Erk ä ltung, H ä nde	like **e** in b **e** d
[ɛ:]	erz äh len, Gespr äch	like **ai** in f **ai** r
[œ]	pl ö tzlich, ö ffnen	somewhere between [ɔ] and [ɛ]
[ø]	nerv ö s, S ö hne	somewhere between [o:] and [e:]
[ʏ]	M ü tter, m ü ssen	similar to [y:] but shorter and with the mouth a bit more open
[y:]	Gem ü se, fr ü her	formed like [i:] but with the lips shaped as for [u:]

Consonants

SYMBOL	EXAMPLE	PRONUNCIATION
[ç]	i ch , wel ch e	no English equivalent, can occur as an allophone of [h] in front of vowels (like **h** uge or **h** ue)

SYMBOL	EXAMPLE	PRONUNCIATION
[ıç]	weni **g**	only as a word ending
[x]	Na **ch** t, au **ch**	after German **a, o, u, au** – no English equivalent, like the Scottish **ch** in lo **ch**
[f]	**f** ünf, **V** ater	like the English **f**
[j]	**j** a, **J** acke	like **y** in New **Y** ork
[k]	Ja **ck** e, we **g**	like **ck** in ja **ck** et
[ŋ]	lä **ng** er	like **ng** in lo **ng**
[p]	**P** ause, gi **b**	like the English **p**
[r]	**r** ot	no English equivalent, like the Scottish **r** in cu **r** d
[e]	Lehr **er**	similar to the English **u** in b **u** t
[z]	le **s** en	like **z** in **z** ero
[s]	Wa **ss** er, Stra **ß** e	like **s** in **s** ay
[ʃ]	**sch** warz	like **sh** in **sh** ow
[ʃp], [ʃt]	**Sp** ort, **st** udieren	combination of [ʃ] and [p] or [t] when **sp** and **st** are combined at the beginning of a word
[t]	gu **t**, Stad **t**, wir **d**	like the English **t**
[tʃ]	deu **tsch**	like **ch** in **ch** at
[v]	**w** irklich	like **v** in **v** oice
[ts]	**Z** immer, pu **tz** en	like **ts** in le **t's**

SOME PRONUNCIATION RULES

[:] means that the previous vowel is a long vowel.

A lot of consonants (b, d, g, h, k, l, m, n, p, t) are generally pronounced the same (or almost the same) as their English counterparts.

Vowels in front of double consonants are always short: Tre **pp** e, pa **ss** ieren.

Double vowels, ie and vowels + h are always long: Tee, passieren, sehr.

b, d, g at the end of a word are pronounced like p, t, k: weg, gib, wird.

h after a vowel is not pronounced. It just prolongs the vowel: Bahn, sehr, wohnen, Uhr.

The German [r] is formed in the throat and pronounced as if you are clearing your throat or gurgling.

STRESS

Usually the first syllable in a word is stressed. However, the stress in German is relatively free and similar looking words can be stressed differently. The primary stress is signalled with ['] the secondary with [,].

ich

[ɪç] *pron*

I

Ich weiß, dass
ich nichts weiß.

*I know that
I know nothing.*

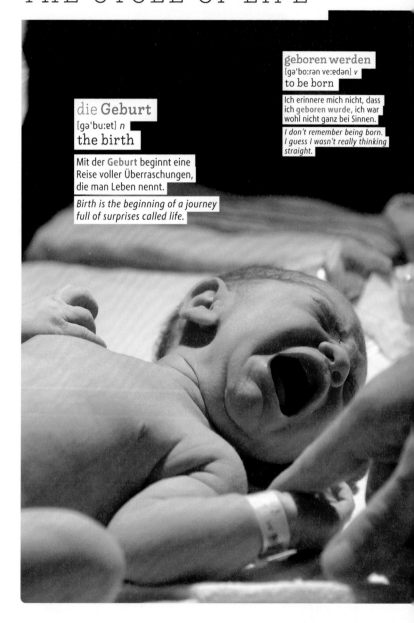

die **Geburt**
[gəˈbuːɐt] *n*
the birth

Mit der Geburt beginnt eine
Reise voller Überraschungen,
die man Leben nennt.

Birth is the beginning of a journey
full of surprises called life.

geboren werden
[gəˈboːrən veːɐdən] *v*
to be born

Ich erinnere mich nicht, dass
ich geboren wurde, ich war
wohl nicht ganz bei Sinnen.

I don't remember being born.
I guess I wasn't really thinking
straight.

das **Baby**
['beːbi] *n*
the baby

Solange es schläft, ist es das
süßeste Baby der Welt.

*As long as it's asleep, it's the
sweetest baby in the world.*

aufwachsen
['aufvaksən] *v*
to grow up

Er ist mit Tieren aufgewachsen.

He's grown up with animals.

der **Junge**
['juŋə] *n*
the boy

das **Mädchen**
['mɛːtçən] *n*
the girl

Manchmal ist es nicht so
einfach zu unterscheiden, wer
Junge und wer Mädchen ist.

*Sometimes it's not so easy
to tell boys and girls apart.*

großziehen
['groːstsiːən] *v*
to bring up

Carla wurde zwischen Kaffee-
tasse und Laptop großgezogen.

*Carla was brought up between
coffee cup and laptop.*

das **Kind**
[kɪnt] *n*
the child

Jedes Kind sollte ein
Instrument lernen.

*Every child should learn
an instrument.*

die **Kindheit**
['kɪnthait] *n*
the childhood

Kindheit heißt, mit vollem
Ernst zu spielen.

*Childhood means taking play
absolutely seriously.*

die **Jugend**
['juːɡənt] *n*
the youth

In der Jugend hört man nur,
was man hören will.

*In your youth you only hear
what you want to hear.*

Opa sieht auf dem Foto so jung aus!

... und er ist immer noch nicht alt ...

Grandpa looks so young in the photo!

jung
[jʊŋ] *adj*
young

alt
[alt] *adj*
old

...and he still isn't old...

der Mensch
[mɛnʃ] *n*
man

Und Gott schuf den Menschen nach seinem Ebenbild.
And God created man in his own image.

menschlich
['mɛnʃlɪç] *adj*
human

Irren ist menschlich!
To err is human.

erwachsen
[ɛ'vaksən] *adj*
adult

Erwachsen zu sein heißt nicht, nie mehr kindisch zu sein.
Being adult doesn't have to mean never being childish.

die Frau
['frau] *n*
the woman

Frauen wollen immer nur das eine ...
Women only ever want one thing...

der Mann
[man] *n*
the man

... und Männer das andere.
...and men the other.

... Jahre alt sein
[...'jaːrə alt zaɪn] *v*
to be... years old

Ich bin schon drei Jahre alt!
I'm already three years old!

leben
['leːbən] *v*
to live

Heinz sagt, er will ewig leben ...
Heinz says he wants to live forever...

das Leben
['leːbən] *n*
the life

Ich hab mir mein Leben wirklich anders vorgestellt.
I really thought my life would be different.

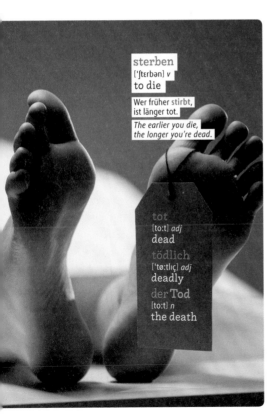

sterben
['ʃtɛrbən] *v*
to die

Wer früher stirbt, ist länger tot.
The earlier you die, the longer you're dead.

tot
[toːt] *adj*
dead

tödlich
['tøːtlɪç] *adj*
deadly

der Tod
[toːt] *n*
the death

lebendig
[leˈbɛndɪç] *adj*
alive

Es hat funktioniert! Es ist lebendig!
It's worked! It's alive!

das Grab
[ɡʁaːp] *n*
the grave

Das Grab meines Urgroßvaters ist in der dritten Reihe.
The grave of my great-grandfather is in the third row.

THE BODY

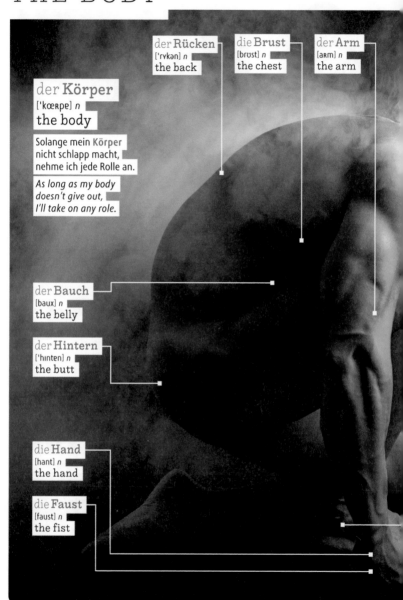

der Rücken
['rʏkən] *n*
the back

die Brust
[brʊst] *n*
the chest

der Arm
[aʀm] *n*
the arm

der Körper
['kœʀpɐ] *n*
the body

Solange mein Körper
nicht schlapp macht,
nehme ich jede Rolle an.

*As long as my body
doesn't give out,
I'll take on any role.*

der Bauch
[baux] *n*
the belly

der Hintern
['hɪntɐn] *n*
the butt

die Hand
[hant] *n*
the hand

die Faust
[faust] *n*
the fist

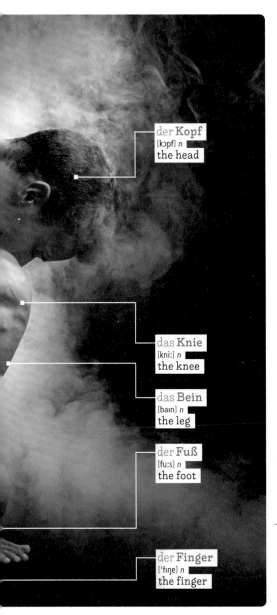

der **Kopf**
[kɔpf] *n*
the head

das **Knie**
[kni:] *n*
the knee

das **Bein**
[baɪn] *n*
the leg

der **Fuß**
[fu:s] *n*
the foot

der **Finger**
['fɪŋɐ] *n*
the finger

das **Blut**
[blu:t] *n*
the blood

Jetzt könnte ich auch ein
Schlückchen Blut vertragen.
*I could do with a little drop
of blood now too.*

das **Herz**
[hɛrts] *n*
the heart

Wer braucht ein Herz, wenn ein
Herz gebrochen werden kann?
*Who needs a heart when a
heart can be broken?*

der **Knochen**
['knɔxən] *n*
the bone

Ein Mensch hat 206 Knochen
im Körper. Für mich reicht einer.
*Humans have 206 bones in their
bodies. One is enough for me.*

das Gehirn
[gə'hɪrn] *n*
the brain

Das menschliche Gehirn
ist zu den erstaunlichsten
Leistungen fähig.

*The human brain is capable
of the most amazing feats.*

die Zunge
['tsʊŋə] *n*
the tongue

Man hat damit ein ganz
anderes Gefühl auf der Zunge.

*It gives you a totally different
feeling on your tongue.*

der Zahn
[tsaːn] *n*
the tooth

Tatsächlich, da fehlt ein Zahn!
There really is a tooth missing!

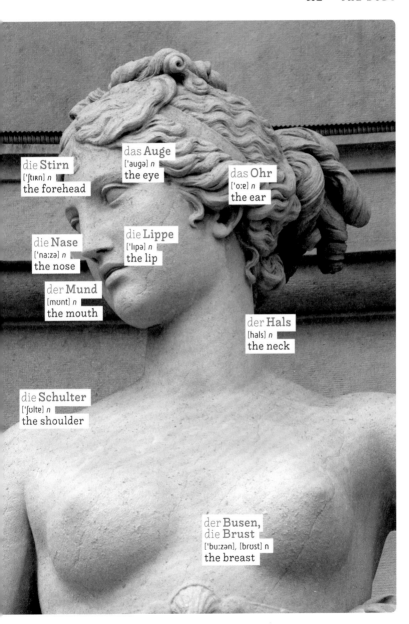

die **Stirn**
['ʃtɪʁn] *n*
the forehead

das **Auge**
['augə] *n*
the eye

das **Ohr**
['oːɐ] *n*
the ear

die **Nase**
['naːzə] *n*
the nose

die **Lippe**
['lɪpə] *n*
the lip

der **Mund**
[mʊnt] *n*
the mouth

der **Hals**
[hals] *n*
the neck

die **Schulter**
['ʃʊltɐ] *n*
the shoulder

der **Busen,**
die **Brust**
['buːzən], [brʊst] *n*
the breast

die **Schönheit**
['ʃøːnhaɪt] *n*
the beauty

Schönheit ist Macht,
ein Lächeln ihr Schwert.

*Beauty is power,
a smile its sword.*

das **Gesicht**
[gə'zɪçt] *n*
the face

Mach nicht so ein
komisches Gesicht.

*Stop pulling such a
funny face.*

schlank
[ʃlaŋk] *adj*
slim

Ja, er ist schlank, das ist aber
auch schon alles.

*Yes, he's slim, but that's
all he is.*

ähneln
['ɛːnəln] *v*
to look alike

Von Nahem ähneln sie sich
gar nicht mehr so sehr.

*They don't look alike quite
so much from close up.*

das **Haar**
[haːɐ] *n*
the hair

Mädchen, schüttle deine Haare für mich!

Girl, shake out your hair for me!

dick
[dɪk] *adj*
fat

dünn
[dʏn] *adj*
thin

Ob dick oder dünn, beide sind meine Freunde.

Fat or thin, both of them are my friends.

Haar is used mostly in the plural in German: Sie hat blonde Haare – "She's got blonde hair." Das Haar (singular) mostly refers to one single hair.

die **Frisur**
[fri'zuːɐ] *n*
the haircut

Vorsicht, mein Anwalt ist auf ruinierte Frisuren spezialisiert!

Be careful, my lawyer specializes in ruined haircuts.

hübsch
[hʏpʃ] *adj*
pretty

Sie sieht hübsch aus in ihrem neuen Kleid.

She looks pretty in her new dress.

klein
[klaɪn] *adj*
short

groß
[groːs] *adj*
tall

Wenn du nicht so klein wärst, kämest du besser ran. – Ach was, du bist einfach zu groß.

If you weren't so short, you'd be able to reach better. – No, you're just too tall.

hässlich
['hɛslɪç] *adj*
ugly

Mama, mit der hässlichen Krawatte geh' ich nicht mit.

Mum, I'm not going with you in this ugly tie.

der **Charakter**
[ka'rakte] *n*
the character

Sie war weder reich
noch berühmt, aber
sie hatte Charakter.

*She was neither rich
nor famous, but she
had character.*

fröhlich
['frø:lɪç] *adj*
cheerful

Um fröhlich zu sein, braucht es keinen Grund.

Who needs a reason to be cheerful?

brav
[bra:f] *adj*
good

Sei ein braves Mädchen und iss deine Karotten.

Be a good girl and eat your carrots.

die Geduld
[gə'dʊlt] *n*
the patience

Der Löwe zeigte viel Geduld mit dem Dompteur.

The lion showed a lot of patience with the lion tamer.

geduldig
[gə'dʊldɪç] *adv*
patiently

Geduldig wartete er auf seine Frau.

He was waiting patiently for his wife.

der Mut
[mu:t] *n*
the courage

Oben angekommen, verließ mich der Mut.

My courage failed me when I got to the top.

ungeduldig
['ʊngədʊldɪç] *adj*
impatient

Langsam werd' ich ungeduldig.

I'm starting to get impatient.

mutig
['mu:tɪç] *adj*
brave

Ist sie mutig oder einfach nur doof?

Is she brave or just stupid?

unhöflich
['ʊnhøːflɪç] *adj*
impolite

Egal, wie Tante Annas Kekse schmecken, das ist einfach unhöflich!

It doesn't matter what Aunt Anna's biscuits taste like, it's just impolite!

lustig
['lʊstɪç] *adj*
funny

Er versuchte verzweifelt, lustig zu sein.

He desperately tried to be funny.

ernst
[ɛrnst] *adv*
seriously

Musst du immer alles so ernst nehmen?

Do you always have to take everything so seriously?

höflich
['høːflɪç] *adj*
polite

Er war so unglaublich höflich, da konnte ich nicht widerstehen.

He was so incredibly polite that I couldn't resist.

neugierig
['nɔygiːrɪç] *adj*
curious

Wer nicht neugierig ist, schafft den Durchbruch nie.

If you aren't curious, you'll never make that breakthrough.

vorsichtig
['foːezɪçtɪç] *adj*
careful

Mein Schatz ist ein vorsichtiger Fahrer.

My darling is a careful driver.

dumm
[dʊm] *adj*
stupid

Ich bin einfach zu **dumm** für diese blöden Hausaufgaben.

I'm just too stupid for this silly homework.

die Dummheit
['dʊmhaɪt] *n*
the stupidity

Und jetzt trittst du auch noch rein. Was für eine **Dummheit**!

And now you're stepping in it too! What stupidity!

unvorsichtig
['ʊnfoːɛzɪçtɪç] *adj*
careless

Du musst diesen **unvorsichtigen** Babysitter sofort rausschmeißen!

You have to fire that careless babysitter immediately!

faul
[faul] *adj*
lazy

Ja, ich bin **faul**. Na und?

Yes, I'm lazy. So what?

ruhig
[ʀuːɪç] *adj*
calm

Wie kannst du da so **ruhig** bleiben? Ich bin schwanger!

How can you keep so calm? I'm pregnant!

lieb, nett
[liːp], [nɛt] adj
kind, nice

Hanna war heute besonders **lieb** zu ihrer Schwester.

Hanna was particularly kind to her sister today.

das **Gefühl**
[gəˈfyːl] *n*
the feeling

Wahre **Gefühle** kann man
nicht unterdrücken.

*There's no way you can
suppress your true feelings.*

mögen
['mø:gən] *v*
to like

Ich **mag** es, schnell ins Büro zu kommen.

I like to get to the office quickly.

die **Freude**
['frɔydə] *n*
the pleasure

Es war so eine **Freude**, Elena ohne ihre Kinder zu sehen.

It was such a pleasure to see Elena without her children.

die **Überraschung**
[y:bɛ'raʃʊŋ] *n*
the surprise

Zu meiner **Überraschung** hatte meine Freundin eine kleine Party organisiert.

To my surprise my girlfriend had organized a little party.

Angst haben (vor)
['aŋst ha:bən (fɔr)] *v*
to fear sth.,
to be afraid (of),

Wovor **hast** du **Angst**? Das ist doch nur ein winziges Tierchen!

What is there to fear? It's just a tiny bug.

wie
[vi:] *prep*
like

Hier fühle ich mich **wie** im Paradies.

I feel like I'm in paradise here.

zufrieden
[tsu:'fri:dən] *adj*
satisfied

Sie haben mir das Kleid umgetauscht, jetzt bin ich **zufrieden**.

They have exchanged the dress, now I'm satisfied.

nicht leiden können
[nɪçt 'laɪdən kœnən] *v*
can't stand

Ich kann dich echt **nicht leiden**!

I really can't stand you!

schrecklich
['ʃrɛklɪç] *adj*
terrible

Das Hotel war einfach **schrecklich**!

The hotel was simply terrible!

die Trauer
['traue] *n*
the mourning

Ihre Trauer hielt sich ziemlich in Grenzen.

Her mourning was pretty restrained.

glücklich sein
['ɡlʏklɪç zaɪn] *v*
to be happy

Ich bin so glücklich, dass es schon wehtut.

I'm so happy it hurts.

Lieblings-
['liːblɪŋs] *adj*
favourite

Das gibt's doch nicht! Die klauen gerade mein Lieblingsauto!

I don't believe it! They're stealing my favourite car!

Ich bin froh, dass der Blumenladen noch offen hatte.

froh
[froː] *adj*
glad

I'm glad that the flower shop was still open.

das Lächeln
['lɛçəln] *n*
the smile

Ein einziges Lächeln kann einem den ganzen Tag retten!

A single smile can make your whole day.

weinen
['vaɪnən] *v*
to cry

Wenn Sam Frodo ins Wasser nachläuft, muss ich immer weinen.

I always have to cry when Sam runs into the water after Frodo.

unangenehm
['ʊn|angəneːm] *adj*
unpleasant

Das könnte ziemlich unangenehm werden.

This could get rather unpleasant.

lachen
['laxən] *v*
to laugh

Über so einen Blödsinn könnt ihr Typen lachen!

That you guys can laugh at such nonsense!

traurig
['traurɪç] *adj*
sad

Sei nicht traurig. Nächstes Jahr steigt ihr wieder auf.

Don't be sad. You'll get promoted again next year.

einsam
['aɪnzaːm] *adj*
lonely

Zurück im Hotel, fühlte Aisha sich wieder furchtbar einsam.

Back in the hotel, Aisha felt awfully lonely again.

unglücklich
['ʊnglʏklɪç] *adj*
unhappy

(sich) fühlen
[(zɪç) 'fyːlən] *v*
to feel

überrascht sein
[yːbe'raʃt zaɪn] *v*
to be surprised

Glück haben
['glʏk haːbən] *v*
to be lucky

die Angst
[aŋst] *n*
the fear

angenehm
['angəneːm] *adj*
pleasant

lächeln
['lɛçəln] *v*
to smile

das Lachen
['laxən] *n*
the laughter

die Traurig-keit
['traurɪçkaɪt] *n*
the sadness

die **Erinnerung**
[ɛɐˈɪnərʊŋ] *n*
the memory

Einen Moment – die Erinnerung kommt gerade wieder.

Hold on – the memory is just coming back to me.

denken
[ˈdɛŋkən] *v*
to think

Was denkst du eigentlich, wer du bist?

Who do you actually think you are?

halten von
[ˈhaltən fɔn] *v*
to think of

Nur eine kurze Frage: Was halten Sie von Heimarbeit?

Just a quick question: what do you think of working from home?

wissen
[ˈvɪsən] *v*
to know

Man sollte immer genau wissen, was man tut …

You should always know exactly what you are doing…

vergessen
[fɛɐˈɡɛsən] *v*
to forget

Tja, die hab' ich vergessen – nun kann ich sie wohl vergessen.

Well, I forgot this one – seems like I can forget about it now.

sich fragen
[zɪç ˈfraːɡən] *v*
to wonder

Ich frage mich, wie das je funktionieren soll.

I wonder how this is ever going to work.

der **Gedanke**
[gə'daŋkə] *n*
the thought

My haircut sucks!

*That's what I wanted to say.
Can he read my thoughts?*

Das wollte
ich gerade
sagen. Kann
er Gedanken
lesen?

Mein Haar-
schnitt ist
voll ätzend!

bemerken
[bə'mɛrkən] *v*
to notice

Zum Glück hat sie mich
noch nicht bemerkt.

*Fortunately she hasn't
noticed me yet.*

erwarten
[ɛɐ'vartən] *v*
to expect

Nein! Das hätte ich wirklich
nie erwartet!

*No! I'd really never have
expected that!*

sich erinnern
[zɪç ɛɐ|'ɪnɐn] *v*
to remember

An das Auto kann ich mich erinnern, an seinen Namen nicht.

*I remember the car but not
his name.*

sehen
['ze:ən] *v*
to see

Manchmal ist es ganz gut, nicht alles scharf zu sehen.

Sometimes it's quite good not to see everything clearly.

schauen
['ʃauən] *v*
to look

Jäger, die schauen, schießen nicht.

Hunters who are looking aren't shooting.

der Blick
[blɪk] *n*
the look

Wenn Blicke töten könnten …

If looks could kill…

hören
['høːʀən] *v*
to hear

Schrei mich nicht an, ich höre noch sehr gut.

Don't shout. I can still hear very well.

das Geräusch, der Klang
[gəˈʀɔyʃ], [klaŋ] *n*
the sound

Schallwellen werden erst zu Klang, wenn ein Ohr da ist.

Sound waves only become sound if there's an ear present.

berühren
[bəˈʀyːʀən] *v*
to touch

Ich mag es, wenn du mich berührst.

I like it when you touch me.

der Geruch
[gəˈʀʊx] *n*
the smell

Mehr und mehr fasziniert mich dieser Geruch.

I'm finding this smell more and more fascinating.

riechen
['riːçən] *v*
to smell

Aber sie muss doch riechen!

But it must smell!

stinken
['ʃtɪŋkən] *v*
to stink

Thomas meint, es stinkt.
Ich finde, er übertreibt.

Thomas thinks it stinks.
I think he's exaggerating.

glauben
['ɡlaʊbən] *v*
to believe

Ich muss nur fest genug dran
glauben …

I only have to believe it
hard enough…

Langsamer,
Mädels – hört
der Musik zu!

zuhören
['tsuːhøːrən] *v*
to listen

Slow down, girls –
listen to the music!

hoffen
['hɔfən] *v*
to hope

Ich hoffe, der Gehweg wird
endlich mal repariert.

I hope they're finally going
to repair the pavement.

annehmen, vermuten
['anneːmən], [fɛɐ'muːtən] *v*
to suppose

Man könnte annehmen,
sie will was von mir.

You might suppose
she was after something.

der Eindruck
['aɪndrʊk] *n*
the impression

Immer dran denken: Der erste
Eindruck zählt!

Always remember. It's the first
impression that counts!

tun
[tu:n] *v*
to do

machen
['maxən] *v*
to do, to make

Was zur Hölle tust du
denn da? Ich dachte, du
machst das Abendessen!

*What the hell are you
doing? I thought you
were making dinner!*

The verb *tun* is often
combined with adjec-
tives to form phrases:
Das tut weh (That
hurts). Otherwise, the
verb *machen* is a com-
mon way of expressing
"to do" in German:
*Ich mache meine Haus-
aufgaben* (I'm doing
my homework).

lassen
['lasən] *v*
to let

Lass los! – Aber lass es mich doch wenigstens angucken ...
Let go! – But let me at least have a look at it first...

hereinkommen, eintreten
[hɛ'raɪn|kɔmən], ['aɪn|tre:tən *v*
to come in

Kommen Sie nur herein!
Just come in!

bewegen
[bə've:gən] *v*
to move

Wenn du ihn fangen willst, musst du dich mehr bewegen!
If you want to catch it, you'll have to move a bit faster!

verlassen
[fɛe'lasən] *v*
to leave

Er verließ sie ohne ein Wort, aber mit großem Getöse.
He left her without a word but with a huge roar.

das Ding
[dɪŋ] *n*
the thing

Das Ding aus dem All.
The thing from outer space.

verwenden, benutzen
[fɛe'vɛndən], [bə'nʊtsən] *v*
to use

Bitte das hier verwenden!
Use this please!

nützlich sein
['nʏtslɪç zaɪn] *v*
to be of use

Ist das Klopapier aus, sind Taschentücher sehr nützlich.
When you've run out of toilet paper, tissues are of enormous use.

die Tätigkeit
['tɛ:tɪçkaɪt] *n*
the activity

die Handlung
['handlʊŋ] *n*
the action

die Sache
['zaxə] *n*
the thing; the matter

der Gegenstand
['ge:gənʃtant] *n*
the object

kommen
['kɔmən] v
to come

Komm endlich rein und mach die Tür zu.

Come on in and close the door.

gehen
['ge:ən] v
to walk, to go

Lasst uns ein bisschen schneller **gehen**.

Let's walk a little faster.

tragen
[tʀaːgən] v
to carry

Vorsicht, er **trägt** eine Waffe!

Watch out! He's carrying a gun!

ziehen
['tsiːən] v
to pull

Und nun **ziehen** wir die Ringe hoch bis unter die Decke …

And now we're going to pull the rings up to the ceiling…

schieben
['ʃiːbən] v
to push

Schauen Sie nicht nur zu, helfen Sie schieben!

Don't just stand there watching, come and help us push!

drücken, pressen
['drʏkən], ['prɛsən] v
to press

Am liebsten würde ich jetzt den Not-Aus-Knopf drücken.

Most of all right now I'd like to press the emergency stop button!

legen
['leːgən] v
to put

Gut, ich lege noch einen drauf. – Ein Haus wird trotzdem nicht draus.

All right. I'll put one more on top. – It's still not going to be a house.

sich umdrehen
[zɪç 'ʊmdreːən] v
to turn (around)

Sie drehte sich zu mir um, lächelte – und schon krachte es.

She turned to me and smiled – and that's when the crash occurred.

halten
['haltən] v
to hold

Nur ich darf unsere Katze halten. Alle anderen kratzt sie.

I'm the only person allowed to hold our cat. It scratches everyone else.

vorbereiten
['foːʁəbaʁaɪtən] v
to prepare

Du wolltest doch das Seil vorbereiten!

You were the one who wanted to prepare the rope!

versuchen
[fɛɐ̯'zuːxən] v
to try

Wenn du es nur oft genug versuchst, schaffst du es auch.

If you try enough times, you'll succeed.

sicher, gewiss
['zɪçɐ], [gə'vɪs] *adj*
sure, certain

Ich bin mir nicht sicher, ob er der Vater ist …

I'm not sure if he's the father...

die Anstrengung
['anʃtrɛŋʊŋ] *n*
the effort

Das richtige Ziel ist jede Anstrengung wert.

The right goal is worth every effort.

die Entscheidung
[ɛnt'ʃaɪdʊŋ] *n*
the decision

Diese Entscheidung will gut überlegt sein.

This decision needs careful consideration.

Als nächsten Schritt planen wir, alle Wände gelb zu streichen.

planen
['plaːnən] *v*
to plan

As our next step we're planning to paint all the walls yellow.

wahrscheinlich
[vaːɐ'ʃaɪnlɪç] *adv*
probably

Ich komme wahrscheinlich ein paar Minuten später.

I'm probably going to be a couple of minutes late.

entscheiden
[ɛnt'ʃaɪdən] *v*
to decide

die Sicherheit, die Gewissheit
['zɪçɐhaɪt], [gə'vɪshaɪt] *n*
the certainty

möglich
['møːklɪç] *adj*
possible

vielleicht
[fi'laɪçt] *adv*
maybe, perhaps

unmöglich
[ʊnˈmøːklɪç] *adj*
impossible

Ich hab's dir gesagt: Damit kann man unmöglich Geld verdienen.

I told you. It's impossible to make money doing that.

suchen
[ˈzuːxən] *v*
to look for, to search

Wenn ich nur wüsste, wonach wir überhaupt suchen.

If only I knew what we're looking for.

finden
[ˈfɪndən] *v*
to find

Ätsch, ihr könnt mich gar nicht finden!

Ha-ha! Bet you can't find me!

entfernen, wegnehmen
[ɛntˈfɛrnən], [ˈvɛkneːmən] *v*
to remove

Ich hätte mir meine Haare doch nicht entfernen lassen sollen.

I shouldn't have got my hair removed.

brauchen
[ˈbrauxən] *v*
to need

Ich brauche noch fünf Minuten …

I just need another five minutes…

schlafen
[ʃla:fən] *v*
to sleep

Lieber acht Stunden Arbeit,
als gar nicht schlafen.

*I'd rather do eight hours of
work than not sleep at all.*

einschlafen
[aɪnʃla:fən] *v*
to fall asleep

Er war so langweilig,
ich bin fast eingeschlafen.

*He was so boring, I nearly fell
asleep.*

wecken
[ˈvɛkən] *v*
to wake

Ich hab' eine todsichere
Methode, Papa zu wecken.

*I've got a sure-fire way
of waking Dad.*

müde
[ˈmy:də] *adj*
tired

Ach, geht doch rüber zu den
Zebras, ich bin jetzt müde.

*Oh, go over and look at the
zebras. I'm tired now.*

aufwachen
[ˈaufvaxən] *v*
to wake up

Feierabend. Zeit, aufzuwachen.

*Time to finish work. Time to
wake up.*

aufstehen
[ˈaufʃte:ən] *v*
to get up

Wenn Leopold mit so guter
Laune aufsteht, ist er
unerträglich.

*Leopold's unbearable when he
gets up in such a good mood.*

besitzen
[bə'zɪtsən] v
to own

So ein Boot wollte ich schon immer besitzen.

I've always wanted to own a boat like that.

eigen
['aɪgən] adj
own

Endlich meine eigene Wohnung!

At last my own flat!

behalten
[bə'haltən] v
to keep

Papa, bitte, können wir ihn behalten?

Dad, please can we keep him?

der **Besitz**,
das **Eigentum**
[bə'zɪts], ['aɪgəntu:m] n
the property

Endlich Eigentum:
Mein eigenes Stück Land!

Some property at last.
My own piece of land!

geben
['ge:bən] *v*
to give

Gib MIR den Teddy!
Give the teddy to ME!

bekommen
[bə'kɔmən] *v*
to get

Arbeitsteilung: Er **bekommt** die Schläge, ich das Geld.

Division of labour: he gets the punches and I get the money.

(mit)bringen
['(mɪt)brɪŋən] *v*
to bring (along)

Bringen Sie ruhig Ihre Freundin **mit**.

Feel free to bring your girlfriend along too.

annehmen
['anne:mən] *v*
to accept

Das kann ich unmöglich **annehmen**.

I couldn't possibly accept it.

erhalten
[ɛɐ'haltən] *v*
to receive, to get

Haben Sie nicht gestern schon Schuhe **bekommen**?

Didn't you receive some shoes just yesterday?

nehmen
['ne:mən] *v*
to take

Geben ist seliger denn **nehmen**.

It is better to give than to take.

mitnehmen
['mɪtneːmən] v
to take (along)

Kannst du auch meinen Liege-
stuhl mitnehmen, Schatz?

*Can you take my deckchair too,
honey?*

haben
[haːbən] v
to have (got)

Seit heute habe ich einen
richtig guten Freund.

*From now on I've got a really
good friend.*

*Haben is also an auxi-
liary verb to indicate
the present perfect of
many verbs: Ich habe
neue Teller gekauft –
"I have bought some
new plates."
A synonym of haben
as a full verb is besit-
zen (to possess).*

auch
[aux] adv
also, too

Zum Burger brauch
ich auch 'ne Cola.

*I also need some cola
with my burger.*

trennen
['trɛnən] v
to separate

Alles, was trennt, kann
überwunden werden.

*Everything that separates can
be overcome.*

reichen
['raɪçən] v
to pass

Würden Sie mir bitte
den Ball reichen?

*Would you please
pass me the ball?*

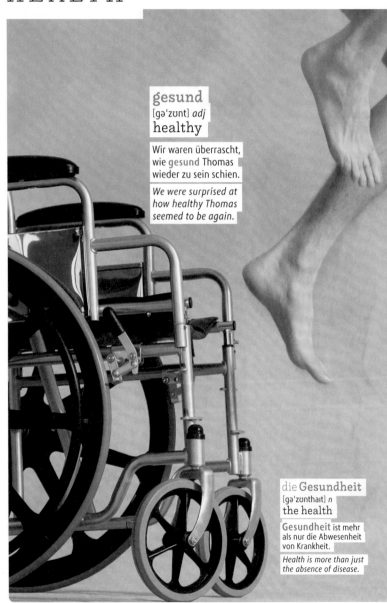

gesund
[gə'zʊnt] *adj*
healthy

Wir waren überrascht, wie gesund Thomas wieder zu sein schien.

We were surprised at how healthy Thomas seemed to be again.

die Gesundheit
[gə'zʊnthaɪt] *n*
the health

Gesundheit ist mehr als nur die Abwesenheit von Krankheit.

Health is more than just the absence of disease.

behindert
[bə'hɪndet] *adj*
disabled

Papa ist doch nicht **behindert**.
Er sitzt nur im Rollstuhl.

Dad isn't disabled.
He just uses a wheelchair.

geistig, psychisch
['gaɪstɪç], ['psy:çɪʃ] *adj*
mental

Ich bin im vollen Besitz
meiner **geistigen** Kräfte.

I'm in full possession
of my mental faculties.

körperlich
['kœrpelɪç] *adj*
physical

An **körperlicher** Präsenz
fehlt es ihm wirklich nicht.

He really doesn't lack
any physical presence.

sich fühlen
[zɪç 'fy:lən] *v*
to feel

Ich **fühl' mich** gut – trotz
Heuschnupfen!

I feel good – despite my
hayfever.

der Schmerz
[ʃmɛrts] *n*
the pain

Gegen diesen **Schmerz** ist
kein Kraut gewachsen.

There's no remedy for
pain like this.

sich verletzen
[zɪç fɛɐ'lɛtsən] *v*
to hurt oneself

Ruf den Notarzt, ich **habe**
mich verletzt!

Call the emergency
doctor, I've hurt myself!

wehtun, schmerzen
[ve: tu:n], ['ʃmɛrtsən] *v*
to hurt

Es tat richtig **weh**, aber er hat
mich überhaupt nicht beachtet.

It really hurt but he completely
ignored me.

gut gehen
['gu:t ge:ən] *v*
to be well

Geht's dem Kind **gut, geht's**
auch der Mutter **gut.**

If the child is well, so is the
mother.

bluten
['blu:tən] v
to bleed

Sie blutete dann doch weniger, als ich gedacht hatte.

She bled less than I'd thought after all.

schlecht, übel
[ʃlɛçt], ['y:bəl] adj
sick

Bei diesem Grün kann einem ja nur übel werden.

That green would make anyone feel sick.

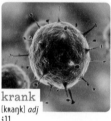

krank
[kraŋk] adj
ill

Diese komischen Auswüchse machen mir Sorgen. Bin ich krank?

I'm worried about these strange growths. Am I ill?

die Kopfschmerzen
['kɔpfʃmɛrtsən] n
the headache

Wenn ich nur wüsste, wo meine Kopfschmerzen herkommen.

If only I knew where I get my headaches from?

leiden
['laɪdən] v
to suffer

Alexander leidet auf hohem Niveau.

Alexander is suffering in style.

husten
['hu:stən] v
to cough

Immer wenn er cool sein wollte, musste er husten.

Whenever he wanted to appear cool, he needed to cough.

sich erkälten
[zɪç ɛɐ'kɛltən] v
to catch a cold

Bei so einem Freund ist es leicht, sich zu erkälten.

It's easy to catch a cold from a friend like that.

schwitzen
['ʃvɪtsən] v
to sweat

Die Hölle, das sind die anderen.
Vor allem, wenn sie schwitzen.

Hell is other people.
Especially when they sweat.

atmen
['a:tmən] v
to breathe

Seit die Kinder bei Harry leben,
kann ich wieder frei atmen.

Since the children started
living with Harry, I've been
able to breathe freely again.

gesund werden
[gə'zʊnt 'vɛrdən] v
to recover

Natürlich wirst du wieder
gesund – irgendwann.

Of course you'll
recover – sometime.

die Wunde
['vʊndə] n
the wound

Lass mich, Mama, es ist nur eine
Fleischwunde.

Leave me alone, Mum.
It's just a flesh wound.

der Schock
[ʃɔk] n
the shock

Ich bekam einen Schock, als er
plötzlich das Licht anmachte.

I got a shock when he suddenly
turned on the light.

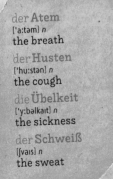

der Atem
['a:təm] n
the breath

der Husten
['hu:stən] n
the cough

die Übelkeit
['y:bəlkaɪt] n
the sickness

der Schweiß
[ʃvaɪs] n
the sweat

bewusstlos
[bə'vʊstlo:s] adj
unconscious

Bewusstlos oder nicht,
wir müssen jetzt los!

Unconcious or not, it's
time we were leaving!

der Zahnarzt, die Zahnärztin
['tsaːnǀaːɛtst], ['tsaːnǀɛːɛtstɪn] *n*
the dentist

Sogar meine Zunge verkrampfte sich, als sie den Zahnarzt sah.

Even my tongue tensed up when it saw the dentist.

verschreiben
[fɛɐ̯'ʃraɪbən] *v*
to prescribe

Ich kann Ihnen da ein fantastisches Mittel verschreiben.

I can prescribe you a fantastic remedy for that.

der Arzt, die Ärztin
['aːɛtst], ['ɛːɛtstɪn] n
the doctor

Teddys Ärztin ist eine echte Spezialistin.

Teddy's doctor is a real specialist.

... Ja, ja, aber in der anderen Apotheke gab's mehr Pröbchen ...

die Apotheke
[apo'teːkə] *n*
the pharmacy

Yes, yes, but at the other pharmacy they had more samples.

medizinisch
[medi'tsiːnɪʃ] *adj*
medical

die Behandlung
[bə'handlʊŋ] *n*
the treatment

das Rezept
[re'tsɛpt] *n*
the prescription

untersuchen
[ʊntɐ'zuːxən] *v*
to examine

die Untersuchung
[ʊntɐˈzuːxʊŋ] *v*
the examination

Seien Sie versichert, diese Untersuchung ist völlig ungefährlich – für mich.

Be assured that this examination is completely safe – for me.

das Medikament
[medikaˈmɛnt] *n*
the medication

Heute möchte ich mal ein anderes Medikament ausprobieren.

Today I'd like to try some different medication.

für
[fyːɐ] *prep*
for

Die rote Hälfte ist für den Magen, die weiße für den Darm.

The red half is for the stomach, the white for the gut.

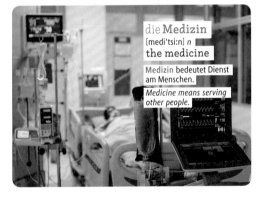

die Medizin
[mediˈtsiːn] *n*
the medicine

Medizin bedeutet Dienst am Menschen.

Medicine means serving other people.

behandeln
[bəˈhandəln] *v*
to treat

Sie fühlte sich gut behandelt.

She felt well treated.

die Vorsorge-untersuchung
[ˈfoːɐzɔrɡəˌʊntɐˈzuːxʊŋ] *n*
the check-up

Glückwunsch, Sie sind meine 500. Vorsorgeuntersuchung!

Congratulations, you're my 500th check-up!

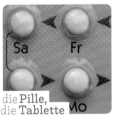

die Pille, die Tablette
[ˈpɪlə], [taˈblɛtə] *n*
the pill, the tablet

Mist, ich habe die Pille schon wieder vergessen.

Damn it, I've forgotten to take the pill again.

der Patient, die Patientin
[pa'tsjɛnt], [pa'tsiɛntɪn] *n*
the patient

Ein Arzt braucht ein enges Verhältnis zu seinen Patienten.

A doctor needs to have a close relationship with his patients.

das Krankenhaus
['kraŋkənhaus] *n*
the hospital

Im Krankenhaus ist just ein Bett frei geworden.

A bed has just become available at the hospital.

die Operation
[opəra'tsjoːn] *n*
the operation

Das ist heute schon meine dritte Operation.

This is already my third operation today.

die Praxis
['praksɪs] *n*
the surgery

Bitte rechnen Sie heute in der Praxis mit längeren Wartezeiten.

Please expect long waiting times at the surgery today.

gefährlich
[gə'fɛːrlɪç] *adj*
dangerous

Gerade eben sah die Piste noch überhaupt nicht gefährlich aus.

Just a moment ago the piste didn't look dangerous at all.

der Krankenwagen
['kraŋkənvaːgən] *n*
the ambulance

Hat dieser Krankenwagen auch WLAN?

Does this ambulance also have Wi-Fi?

retten
['rɛtən] *v*
to save

War nur ein Spaß. Ich rette dich ja gleich.

It was just a bit of fun. I'll save you right away.

die **Kranken-schwester**
['kraŋkənʃvəstɐ] *n*
the nurse

Wirklich? Die Kranken-schwester erbt alles?

Really? The nurse inherits everything?

der **Alarm**
[aˈlarm] *n*
the alarm

Bei Alarm muss das ganze Krankenhaus evakuiert werden.

When the alarm goes off, the whole hospital has to be evacuated.

der **Krankenpfleger**
['kraŋkənpfleːgɐ] *n*
the male nurse

… Und der Krankenpfleger erbt nichts?

…And the male nurse doesn't inherit a thing?

die **Notrufnummer**
['noːtruːfnʊmɐ] *n*
the emergency number

Wählen Sie die Notrufnummer, dann kommen wir auch.

Dial the emergency number and we'll be there.

um Hilfe rufen
[ʊm ˈhɪlfə ruːfən] *phrase*
to call for help

Ruf doch **um Hilfe**, Papa!

Go on, Dad, call for help!

die **Gefahr**
[gəˈfaːɐ] *n*
the danger

die **Klinik**
['kliːnɪk] *n*
the clinic

operieren
[opəˈriːrən] *v*
to operate

Hilfe!
['hɪlfə] *interj*
Help!

CLOTHING

die **Kleider,**
die **Kleidung**
['klaɪdɐ], ['klaɪdʊŋ] *n*
the clothes

Irgendwie stecken wir doch
alle sehr nackt in unseren
Kleidern.

*In a way we're all extremely
naked in our clothes.*

die **Hose**
['hoːzə] *n*
the trousers

das **Hemd**
[hɛmt] *n*
the shirt

das **Kleid**
[klaɪt] *n*
the dress

die **Arm-banduhr**
['armbant|u:ɐ] *n*
the (wrist) watch

der **Ring**
[rɪŋ] *n*
the ring

die **Jacke**
['jakə] *n*
the jacket

die **Jeans**
['dʒi:ns] *n*
the jeans

die **Tasche**
['taʃə] *n*
the bag

die **(Kleider)Größe**
['(klaɪde)grø:sə] *n*
the size

Wunderbar, mein Herr, genau
Ihre Größe!
Excellent, sir. Just your size!

anprobieren
['anprobi:rən] *v*
to try on

Probier mal diesen Hut an ...
Just try this hat on...

passen
['pasən] *v*
to fit

In ein paar Jahren passen
die Schuhe ...
*These shoes will fit in
a couple of years...*

der Rock
[rɔk] *n*
the skirt

In diesem Rock bin ich über
den Atlantik geflogen …

*I flew across the Atlantic
in this skirt…*

der Anzug
['antsuːk] *n*
the suit

Charmant ist er ja, aber sein
Anzug ist aus dem Leihhaus.

*He is charming, but his suit
came from the pawnbroker's.*

der Hut
[huːt] *n*
the hat

Diesen Hut will ich, und sonst
keinen!

I want that hat and no other!

der Mantel
['mantəl] *n*
the coat

Ohne Mantel würde meine Püp-
pi doch so schrecklich frieren.

*My Popsy would be so terribly
cold without her coat.*

der Handschuh
['hantʃuː] *n*
the glove

Mit solchen Handschuhen ist
Putzen das reine Vergnügen.

*Gloves like these make cleaning
a real pleasure.*

der Regenschirm
['reːgənʃirm] *n*
the umbrella

Du hast den Regenschirm
wirklich dem Typ da geklaut?

*You really pinched this umbrella
off that guy over there?*

die Brille
['brɪlə] *n*
the glasses

Hey, ich brauch' ja gar keine
Brille!

*Hey, I don't need
glasses after all!*

der Ohrring
['oːrɪŋ] *n*
the earring

Beim Pfandleiher kriege ich
mindestens 50 Euro für die
Ohrringe!

*I'll get at least 50 euros at the
pawn shop for these earrings!*

die Halskette
['halskɛtə] *n*
the necklace

Die Halskette ist dein,
und du bist mein.

*The necklace is yours,
and you are mine.*

die **Unterhose**
['unteho:zə] *n*
the (pair of) briefs

sich **umziehen**
[zɪç 'ʊmtsi:ən] *v*
to change

Wie lange brauchst du eigentlich, um dich umzuziehen?

How long do you actually need to get changed?

der **Pullover**
[pʊ'lo:vɐ] *n*
the pullover

der **Schuh**
[ʃu:] *n*
the shoe

die **Socke**
['zɔkə] *n*
the sock

die **Bluse**
['blu:zə] *n*
the blouse

eng
[ɛŋ] *adj*
tight

Es war eng, aber wir haben
gewonnen.

It was tight, but we won.

weit
[vaɪt] *adj*
wide

In weiten Hosen zu tanzen
macht doppelt Spaß!

*Dancing in wide trousers
is double the fun!*

kurz
[kʊʁts] *adj*
short

Ihr Rock was so kurz, dass er
schon fast wie ein Gürtel wirkte.

*Her skirt was so short it was
almost a belt.*

Jacke
ausziehen,
Jacke anziehen –
kannst du dich
endlich mal
entscheiden?

lang
[laŋ] *adj*
long

Das Kleid war lang,
die Ehe kurz.

*The dress was long,
the marriage short.*

anziehen
['antsiːən] *v*
to put on

ausziehen
['austsiːən] *v*
to take off

*Put the jacket on,
take the jacket off –
can you finally make
up your mind?*

sich anziehen
[zɪç 'antsiːən] *v*
to put on
one's clothes

sich ausziehen
[zɪç 'austsiːən] *v*
to take off
one's clothes

die **Sonnenbrille**
['zɔnənbrɪlə] *n*
the sunglasses

der **Bikini**
[bi'ki:ni] *n*
the bikini

die **Qualität**
[kvali'tɛ:t] *n*
the quality

Mein Badeanzug-Schneider
liefert nur beste Qualität.

*My swimsuit designer only
delivers the best quality.*

der **Badeanzug**
['ba:dəantsu:k] *n*
the swimsuit

die **Badehose**
['ba:dəho:zə] *n*
the swimming
trunks

tragen, anhaben
[tʀa:gən], ['anha:bən] *v*
to wear

Orange kann man in jedem Alter
tragen.

*You can wear orange no matter
what age you are.*

der **Schlafanzug**
['ʃla:fʃantsu:k] *n*
the pyjamas

Bring mir meinen Schlafanzug,
Xerxes!

Bring me my pyjamas, Xerxes!

das **Nachthemd**
['naxthɛmt] *n*
the nightshirt

Ich kann den Herzog doch nicht
im Nachthemd empfangen.

*I can't receive the duke
in my nightshirt.*

OTHER
PEOPLE

die **anderen**
['andərən] *n*
the others

Ich kann nichts dafür!
Das waren die anderen.

It's not my fault!
It was the others.

die **Großmutter**
['gro:smʊtɐ] *n*
the grandmother

der **Vater**
['fa:tɐ] *n*
the father

die **Tochter**
['dɔːtɐ] *n*
the daughter

der **Sohn**
[zoːn] *n*
the son

die **Familie**
[faˈmiːliə] *n*
the family

Zur Kirschblüte spielen wir
immer „glückliche Familie".

*When it's the cherry blossom
season, we always play
"happy families".*

der **Großvater**
['groːsfatɛ] *n*
the grandfather

die **Mutter**
['mʊtɐ] *n*
the mother

die **Schwester**
['ʃvɛstɐ] *n*
the sister

Meine Schwester ist 'ne
blöde Petze.
*My sister is a stupid
little snitch.*

der **Bruder**
['bruːdɐ] *n*
the brother

Sagt mal, seid ihr Brüder?
Tell me, are you brothers?

die **Mama**
['mama] *n*
the mum

der **Papa**
['papa] *n*
the dad

die **Oma**
['oːma] *n*
the grandma

der **Opa**
['oːpa] *n*
the grandpa

die Eltern
['ɛltən] *n*
the parents

Jedes Jahr schleppen meine Eltern uns an die Nordsee.

Every year, my parents drag us off to the North Sea.

die Tante
['tantə] *n*
the aunt

Unsere Tante bestand auf einem Küsschen.

Our aunt insisted on a kiss.

der Onkel
['ɔŋkəl] *n*
the uncle

Dein Onkel hält sich für einen großen Handwerker, was?

Your uncle reckons himself to be a bit of a handyman, doesn't he?

der Cousin
die Cousine
[ku'zɛ̃], [ku'ziːnə] *n*
the cousin

Cousin, die Ente bleibt draußen!

The duck stays out, cousin!

die Ehefrau
['eːəfrau] *n*
the wife

Wer so eine Ehefrau hat, braucht keine Geliebte.

With a wife like that, you don't need a mistress.

der Ehemann
['eːəman] *n*
the husband

Ein braver Ehemann ist der Traum jeder Schwiegermutter.

A dutiful husband is every mother-in-law's dream.

das Paar
['paːɐ] *n*
the couple

Was für ein schönes Paar!

What a lovely couple!

ledig
['le:dɪç] *adj*
single

Solange ich ledig bleibe, bekommen meine Füße genügend Luft.

My feet will keep getting plenty of air as long as I stay single.

die Hochzeit
['hɔxtsaɪt] *n*
the wedding

Nach der Hochzeit muss ich gleich wieder ins Büro, Schatz.

I need to get straight back to the office after the wedding, darling.

verheiratet
[fɛɛ'haɪra:tət] *adj*
married

Gell, da schaust du: seit 52 Jahren glücklich verheiratet.

Just look at that, happily married for 52 years.

heiraten
[haɪra:tən] *v*
to get married

Was soll ich einen Prinzen heiraten, wenn ich dich haben kann?

Why would I want to get married to a prince when I can have you?

die Liebe
['li:bə] *n*
the love

Blindlings trifft der Liebe Pfeil.
Love is blind.

zusammenleben
[tsu'zamənle:bən] *v*
to live together

Zusammenzuleben *ist nicht immer leicht.*

Living together isn't always easy.

lieben
['li:bən] *v*
to love

Ich liebe das Gefühl von warmem Sand zwischen meinen Zehen.
I love the feel of warm sand between my toes.

der Kuss
[kʊs] *n*
the kiss

Mit so einem Kuss habe ich damals schon Dornröschen geweckt.
I woke Sleeping Beauty with a kiss like this.

(sich) küssen
[zɪç 'kʏsən] *v*
to kiss

Bah, Menschen küssen immer so weich.

Eugh, humans always kiss so softly.

Herr
[hɛr] *n*
Mr

So sehen wir uns wieder,
Herr Bond!

So, we meet again, Mr Bond!

Frau
['frau] *n*
Mrs, Ms

Ich gratuliere zum Gewinn
des Schönheitswettbewerbs
Frau Fu.

*Congratulations on winning
the beauty contest, Mrs Fu.*

The formerly common courtesy title Fräulein to address an unmarried woman is outdated in modern German, similar to the English "Miss".

sich kümmern um
[zɪç 'kʏmən 'ʊm] *v*
to care about

Sie kümmern sich sehr um
Oma, sie besuchen sie
mindestens einmal im Jahr.

*They care about grandma
so much, they visit her
at least once a year.*

treu
[trɔy] *adj*
faithful

Herrchen, wirst du mir immer
treu bleiben?

*Will you always be faithful
to me, master?*

untreu
['ʊntrɔy] *adj*
unfaithful

Bei mir wird garantiert
jede Frau untreu …

*No woman could fail to
be unfaithful with me…*

hassen
['hasən] *v*
to hate

Ich hasse Kürbissuppe zum Frühstück

I hate pumpkin soup for breakfast.

der Hass
[has] *n*
the hatred

Hass geht oft mit Dummheit einher.

Hatred often goes hand in hand with stupidity.

(sich) trennen
[(zɪç) 'trɛnən] *v*
to separate

Vielleicht sollten wir uns trennen …

Perhaps we should separate...

die Witwe
['vɪtvə] *n*
the widow

So jung und schon Witwe!

So young and already a widow!

sich scheiden lassen
[zɪç 'ʃaɪdən 'lasən] *v*
to get divorced

Seit ich mich habe scheiden lassen, schlafen die Kinder wieder ruhig.

The kids have been sleeping better since I got divorced.

der Witwer
['vɪtvɐ] *n*
the widower

Ich wollte, ich könnte den alten Witwer ein wenig aufheitern.

I wished I could do something to cheer the old widower up a bit.

der **Freund**, die **Freundin**
[frɔynt], ['frɔyndɪn] *n*
the friend

Nachdem alle meine Freunde von Bord waren, hatte ich das Boot endlich für mich.

Once all my friends had jumped overboard, I finally had the boat to myself.

der/die **Bekannte**
[bə'kantə] *n*
the acquaintance

Leider ist sie nur eine flüchtige Bekannte.

Sadly, she is just a casual acquaintance.

die **Freundschaft**
['frɔyntʃaft] *n*
the friendship

Erwin und Karl-Heinz verbindet eine tiefe Freundschaft.

Erwin and Karl-Heinz share a close friendship.

freundlich
[frɔyntlɪç] *adj*
friendly

Wir lächelten alle recht freundlich.

We all gave a friendly smile.

PERSONAL PRONOUNS

ich [ɪç] *pron* I	du [duː] *pron* you	Sie [ziː] *pron* you
er [ɛʀ] *pron* he	sie [ziː] *pron* she	es [ɛs] *pron* it
wir [viːɐ] *pron* we	ihr [iːɐ] *pron* you	sie [ziː] *pron* they

persönlich
[pɛɐˈzøːnlɪç] *adj*
personal

Heute möchte ich dir einen persönlichen Brief schreiben.

Today, I'd like to write you a personal letter.

die Leute
[ˈlɔytə] *n*
people

So viele Leute … Lass uns nach Hause gehen.

There are so many people… Let's go home.

der Einwohner, die Einwohnerin
[ˈaɪnvoːne], [ˈaɪnvoːnɐrɪn] *n*
the inhabitant

Nur einer der zehn Millionen Einwohner der Stadt.

Just one of the city's ten million inhabitants.

der Nachbar, die Nachbarin
[ˈnaxbaːe], [ˈnaxbarɪn] *n*
the neighbour

Hast du den neuen Grill vom Nachbarn gesehen?

Have you seen the neighbour's new barbecue?

der Kerl
[kɛrl] *n*
the guy

Leg dich mit dem Kerl lieber nicht an!

I wouldn't pick a fight with that guy if I were you!

zusammen
[tsuˈzamən] *adv*
together

Wir spielen zusammen, aber immer nur „La Cucaracha".

We play together but only "La Cucaracha".

treffen
[ˈtrɛfən] *v*
to meet

Auch aus Köln? Und dann treffen wir uns hier in Sydney?

You're also from Cologne? Fancy us meeting here in Sydney!

das Treffen
[trɛfən] *n*
the gathering

An das Treffen habe ich gar keine Erinnerung mehr.

I have absolutely no recollection of the gathering.

die Versammlung
[fɛɐ'zamlʊŋ] *n*
the meeting

Ich begrüße Sie zur ordentlichen Versammlung des Kaninchen-züchter-Vereins.

Welcome to the regular meeting of the Rabbit Breeders Society.

einladen
['aɪnlaːdən] *n*
to invite

Sara lädt schon wieder Hinz und Kunz ein.

Sara isn't fussy about who she invites over.

besuchen
[bə'zuːxən] *v*
to visit

Dreimal die Woche besuche ich meinen Eduard.

I visit my Eduard three times a week.

der Gast
[gast] *n*
the guest

Die Gäste waren mehr als peinlich!

The guests were so embarrassing!

POSSESSIVE PRONOUNS

mein	**dein**	**Ihr**
[maɪn] *pron*	[daɪn] *pron*	[iːɐ] *pron*
my, mine	your	your
sein	**ihr**	**unser**
[zaɪn] *pron*	[iːɐ] *pron*	['ʊnzɐ] *pron*
his; its	her(s)	our
euer	**ihr**	
['ɔyɐ] *pron*	[iːɐ] *pron*	
your	their	

das **Gespräch**
[gə'ʃprɛːç] *n*
the conversation

Das Gespräch war nett –
bis Julia Herbert erwähnte.

*We were having a perfectly nice
conversation until Julia menti-
oned Herbert.*

erzählen
[ɛɐ'tsɛːlən] *v*
to tell

sagen
[zaːgən] *v*
to say

Die Krähe erzählte von
ihrem Film mit Hitchcock.
Die Kuh sagte nichts.

*The crow was telling
the story of when it was
in Hitchcock's film.
The cow said nothing.*

die **Rede**
['reːdə] *n*
the speech

Wenn du die Rede erst begon-
nen hast, legt sich die Angst.

*Once you've started the speech,
your nerves will vanish.*

nennen
['nɛnən] *v*
to call

Nenn mich nicht Idiot und ruf
mich nie wieder an!

*Don't call me an idiot and
never call me again!*

heißen
['haɪsən] *v*
to be called

Sie heißt Rosie und will
nur spielen.

*She is called Rosie and she
just wants to play.*

still
[ʃtɪl] *adj*
quiet

Es war ein bisschen zu
still am Wasser …

*It was a bit too quiet
down by the water…*

ruhig
[ʀuːɪç] *adj*
calm

Lazio Rom hatte verloren, aber
Antonio blieb erstaunlich ruhig.

*Although Lazio had lost,
Antonio stayed incredibly calm.*

Die **Stille** im Kinderzimmer ist einfach herrlich… aber wir müssen leise sein, sonst wecken wir sie auf!

die **Stille**
['ʃtɪlə] *n*
the silence

leise sein
['laɪzə zaɪn] *v*
to be quiet

*The silence in the children's room is wonderful…
but we need to be quiet or we'll wake them up!*

der **Name**
['naːmə] *n*
the name

Wie war doch gleich der **Name** von diesem Komiker?
What was that comic actor's name again?

Hallo!
[haˈloː] *interj*
Hello!, Hi!

Hallo, sagte er schüchtern.
Hello, he said shyly.

der **Nachname**
['naːxnamə] *n*
the last name

Sehr erfreut! Ist Wang Ihr Vor- oder Ihr **Nachname**?
Pleased to meet you! Is Wang your first name or your last name?

der **Vorname**
['foːenaːmə] *n*
the first name

Schreiben Sie alle **Vornamen** in das dafür vorgesehene Feld.
Write down all your first names in the appropriate box.

Willkommen!
[vɪlˈkɔmən] *interj*
Welcome!

Willkommen in unserer bescheidenen Nudelsuppenbude!
Welcome to our humble little noodle soup joint!

Sehr erfreut!
['zeːɐ ɛɐ'frɔyt] *phrase*
Nice to meet you!

Sehr erfreut!
Ich bin Herr Fischer.

Nice to meet you!
I'm Mr Fisher.

Gute Nacht!
[guːtə 'naxt] *interj*
Good night!

Gute Nacht, Mama und Papa.
Und habt keine Angst, ich bin
ja da.

Good night, Mummy and
Daddy. And don't be afraid,
I'll be here if you need me.

Bis dann!
Bis gleich!
[bɪs 'dan], [bɪs 'glaɪç] *interj*
See you!

Bis dann! Und bring den Hub-
schrauber rechtzeitig zurück!

See you! And make sure
you bring the helicopter back
on time!

Guten Morgen!
[guːtən 'mɔʁgən] *interj*
Good morning

Guten Tag
[guːtən 'taːk] *interj*
Good afternoon!

Guten Abend!
[guːtən 'aːbənt] *interj*
Good evening!

Auf Wiedersehen!
[auf 'viːdeːzeːən] *interj*
Goodbye!!

die **Frage**
['fra:gə] *n*
the question

Sein oder nicht sein, das ist hier die Frage.

To be or not to be, that is the question.

Wie bitte?
['vi: 'bɪtə] *interj*
Pardon?

Wie bitte? Ich denke, die Leitung ist gestört.

Pardon? I think it must be a bad line..

fragen
[fʀa:gən] *v*
to ask

Darf ich Sie noch etwas fragen? Was machen Sie nach dem Unterricht?

Can I ask you something else? What are you doing after class?

bitten
['bɪtən] *v*
to request, to ask

She's asking for the protection of her ancestors.

Sie bittet um den Schutz ihrer Ahnen.

die **Antwort**
['antvɔrt] *n*
the answer

Ich weiß die Antwort!

I know the answer!

oder
['o:de] *conj*
or

Hey, hör mal – sie oder ich!

Hey, listen up, it's me or her!

antworten
['antvɔrtən] *n*
to answer

Hansi antwortet auf jede Frage, aber immer das Gleiche.

Hansi answers any question, but he always says the same thing.

noch einmal
[nɔx ˈaɪnmaːl] *adv*
again

*Spiel's noch einmal, Sam.
Aber diesmal im Rhythmus.*

*Play it again, Sam.
But stay in time this time.*

und
[unt] *conj*
and

Herr Pfeffer und Frau Salz
waren sich auf Anhieb
sympathisch.

*Mr Pepper and Mrs Salt hit
it off right away.*

ja
[jaː] *adv*
yes

Ja, ich will – hättest du dir ja
denken können, bei dem Kleid.

*Yes, I do – what else am I going
to say to you in a dress like that! .*

nicht
[nɪçt] *adv*
not

Ich habe das nicht
bestellt, und ich
finde das absolut
nicht komisch.

*I did not order it and
I certainly don't think
it's funny.*

nein
[naɪn] *adv*
no

Alles, was du sagen kannst,
ist immer nur nein!

All you ever say is no!

Na klar!
[naˈklaːɐ] *interj*
Sure!

Na klar! Bis morgen ist Ihr
Auto fertig.

*Sure! Your car will be ready
by tomorrow.*

Danke...
so eine
schöne
Lupe!

Danke (schön)!
['daŋkə (ʃøːn)] *interj*
Thank you!

*Thank you...
what a lovely
magnifying glass!*

Keine Ursache!
Und wenn du
sie mal nicht
brauchst,
kann ich sie mir
ausleihen...?

Keine Ursache!
['kaɪnə 'uːrzaxə] *interj*
You're welcome!

*You're welcome!
And can I borrow it if
you don't need it...?*

bitte
['bɪtə] *interj*
please

Noch einen Wodka bitte.
Another vodka, please.

wollen
['vɔlən] *v*
to want

Papa, ich will ein Pony.
Biiiiiiitteeeee!
*I want a pony, Dad.
Pleeeease!*

fordern, verlangen
['fɔrdən], [fɛɛ'laŋən] *v*
to demand

Wir fordern mehr Zeit fürs
Demonstrieren.
*We demand more time for
demonstrations.*

versprechen
[fɛɐ'ʃprɛçən] *v*
to promise

Ich verspreche dir, morgen kaufe ich ein neues Auto.

I promise you I'll buy a new car tomorrow.

die Erlaubnis
[ɛɐ'laupnɪs] *n*
the permission

Die Erlaubnis zum Betreten der Damentoilette wurde erteilt.

Permission was granted to enter the ladies' toilet.

der Befehl
[bə'feːl] *n*
the orderl

Über meine Befehle wird nicht diskutiert!

My orders are not up for discussion!

dürfen
['dʏrfən] *v*
to be allowed to

Im Sommer darf ich endlich wieder trinken UND rauchen..

In the summer, I'm finally allowed to drink AND smoke again.

erlauben
[ɛɐ'laubən] *v*
to allow

Meine Lieblinge erlauben mir ab und zu, mich zu ihnen zu setzen.

Sometimes my little darlings allow me to sit with them.

die Forderung
['fɔrdərʊŋ] *n*
the demand

befehlen
[bə'feːlən] *v*
to order

das Versprechen
[fɛɐ'ʃprɛçən] *n*
the promise

verbieten
[fɛɐ'biːtən] *v*
to prohibit

Ein paar Dinge muss man eben verbieten.

There are some things you need to prohibit.

das Verbot
[fɛɐ'boːt] *n*
the ban

Ein Verbot ist für Karl nur ein zusätzlicher Anreiz

For Karl, a ban is just an added incentive.

die **Meinung**
['maɪnʊŋ], ['anzɪçt] *n*
the opinion

Dazu hab' ich absolut keine
Meinung ...

*I have no opinion at all
on the matter...*

ausdrücken
['ausdrʏkən] *v*
to express

Musik ist meine Art,
mich auszudrücken.

*Music is my way of
expressing mysel*

meinen
['maɪnən] *v*
to mean

Meinen Sie mich?
Do you mean me??

**annehmen,
vermuten**
['anne:mən], [fɛɐ'mu:tən] *v*
to suppose

Ich nehme an,
Sie schreiben Ihrem
Ex-Mann ...

*I suppose you're
writing to your ex...*

raten
['ra:tən] *v*
to advise

Ich kann Ihnen nur raten,
Ihre Berater zu wechseln.

*I can only advise you to change
your advisors.*

überzeugen
[y:be'tsɔygən] *v*
to convince

Madame, Sie können wirklich
überzeugen!

*Madam, you certainly know
how to convince people!*

scheinen
['ʃaɪnən] *v*
to seem

Als ich klein war, schien alles
unendlich groß zu sein.

*When I was little, everything
seemed incredibly big.*

verschieden
[fɛɐ̯'ʃiːdən] *adj*
different

gleich
[glaɪç] *adj*
equal

Verschiedene Farben,
gleiches Gewicht..

*Different colours,
equal weight.*

tolerieren
[toleˈriːrən] *v*
to tolerate

Wir tolerieren bei uns auch
schwarze Schafe.

*We tolerate black
sheep, too.*

empfehlen
[ɛmˈpfeːlən] *v*
to recommend

Tadschikistan im Frühling kann
ich wirklich empfehlen.

*I can really recommend
Tajikistan in spring.*

vorschlagen
[ˈfoːɐ̯ʃlaːgən] *v*
to suggest

Eigentlich müsste ich Ihnen
ein anderes Restaurant
vorschlagen.

*I really ought to suggest
a different restaurant.*

zustimmen
[ˈtsuːʃtɪmən] *v*
to agree

Wenn alle zustimmen, bekommt
ihr von mir auch ein „Like".

*If everyone agrees, then I'll
like you, too.*

vorziehen
[ˈfoːɐ̯tsiːən] *v*
to prefer

Ich würde blau vorziehen,
aber beim Bayern-Spiel
geht das nicht.

*I prefer the blue, but I can't
wear that to a Bayern Munich
match.*

das Gegenteil
[ˈgeːgəntaɪl] *n*
the opposite

Ist Tradition wirklich das
Gegenteil von Moderne?

*Is tradition really the opposite
of modernity?*

OK, ich hatte unrecht. Das ist nicht dein Stil.

unrecht haben
['ʊnrɛçt 'ha:bən] *v*
to be wrong

OK, I was wrong.
It isn't your style.

recht haben
['rɛçt ha:bən] *v*
to be right

Du hast recht: Es waren die Deutschen!

You are right. It was the Germans!

der Grund
[grʊnt] *n*
the reason

Ich brauche einen neuen Sessel; der Grund – ist mein Hund!

I need a new chair.
The reason – my dog!

der Unterschied
['ʊntɐʃiːt] *n*
the difference

die Empfehlung
[ɛm'pfeːlʊŋ] *n*
the recommendation

der Vorschlag
['foːɐʃlaːk] *n*
the suggestion

die Einigung
['aɪnɪgʊŋ] *n*
the agreement

helfen
['hɛlfən] v
to help

Vielleicht könntest du auch ein bisschen helfen!

Perhaps you could help a bit, too!

offensichtlich
[ɔfən'zɪçtlɪç] adj
obvious

Du magst Schoko aufs Brot, das ist offensichtlich!

It's obvious you like chocolate spread on your bread!

In Ordnung!
[ɪn 'ɔrdnʊŋ] interj
All right!

Darf's ein bisschen mehr Melone sein? – In Ordnung!

A bit more melon? – All right!

nützlich
['nʏtslɪç] adj
useful

So ein kleiner Schirm kann in vielerlei Weise nützlich sein.

A small umbrella like this can be useful in so many different ways.

klar
[klaːɐ] adj
clear

Jetzt ist die Sache klar.
Everything is clear now.

die Unterstützung
[ʊntɐ'ʃtʏtsʊŋ] n
the support

Danke für deine Unterstützung.
Thanks for your support.

der Gefallen
[gə'falən] *n*
the favour

Tust du mir den Gefallen und schmierst mir den Rücken ein?

Will you do me a favour and put some suntan lotion on my back?

genau
[gə'nau] *adv*
exactly

Tu genau, was ich dir sage, dann triffst du ins Gelbe.

Do exactly what I say and you'll hit the bullseye.

wichtig
['vɪçtɪç] *adj*
importan

Du sagst, der Helm ist wichtig, Mama, aber selber trägst du keinen.

You say the helmet's important, Mum, but you're not wearing one yourself.

das heißt
[das 'haɪst] *phrase*
that is to say

Es gibt also neue Strukturen, **das heißt**: Großraumbüros für alle.

We are restructuring, that is to say there will be open-plan offices for everyone

zum Beispiel
[tsʊm 'baɪʃpiːl] *phrase*
for example

Diese Szene **zum Beispiel** wirkt total künstlich.

This scene, for example, is totally artificial.

kritisieren
[kriti'ziːrən] *v*
to criticize

Genau hinzusehen bedeutet nicht gleich zu kritisieren.

Taking a careful look at something doesn't necessarily mean you have to criticize it.

zwecklos, nutzlos
['tsvɛkloːs], ['nʊtsloːs] *adj*
useless

Es ist zwecklos zu warten. Heute kommt kein Zug mehr.

It's useless waiting. There won't be any more trains today.

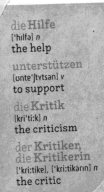

die Hilfe
['hɪlfə] *n*
the help

unterstützen
[ʊntɐ'ʃtʏtsən] *v*
to support

die Kritik
[kri'tiːk] *n*
the criticism

der Kritiker,
die Kritikerin
['kriːtikɐ], ['kriːtikərɪn] *n*
the critic

gegen
['ge:gən] *prep*
against

Ich hab' was gegen Mücken!

I've got something against mosquitoes!!

sauer, ärgerlich
['zauɐ], ['ɛrgɐlɪç] *adj*
annoyed, upset

Bei jeder Kleinigkeit wirst du gleich sauer.

You always get annoyed at the slightest thing.

die Wut
[vu:t] *n*
the rage

Er wirkte stolz und schön in seiner Wut.

His rage made him look proud and beautiful.

sich aufregen
[zɪç 'aufre:gən] *v*
to get upset

Bitte, regen Sie sich nicht auf, ich weiß es einfach nicht.

Please don't get upset, I just don't know.

(sich) streiten
[(zɪç) 'ʃtraɪtən] *v*
to argue, to fight

Lass uns nicht streiten, die Blumen waren teuer.

Let's not argue, the flowers were expensive

wütend
['vy:tənt] *adj*
angry

Wenn Harry wütend wird, bekommt er, was er will.

When Harry gets angry, he always gets his way.

stören
['ʃtø:rən] *v*
to disturb

Bitte nicht stören!

Do not disturb!

der Ärger
['ɛrgɐ] *n*
the trouble

Immer macht mir die Dreckskarre Ärger.

This pile of junk is always giving me trouble.

weil
[vaɪl] *conj*
because

Weil du schon wieder keine
Socken anhast, wirst du
gekitzelt.

*You're going to get tickled
because you haven't got
your socks on again.*

wenn
[vɛn] *conj*
if

Wenn du etwas höher
gesprungen wärst, hättest
du ihn gekriegt.

*You'd have caught it if you'd
jumped a bit higher.*

um … zu, damit
[ʊm … tsuː], [daˈmɪt] *conj*
(in order) to

Um auszusteigen, musst du
den Knopf drücken.

*To get out, you need to press
the button.*

**der Streit,
die Auseinandersetzung**
[ʃtraɪt], [ausǀaɪˈnandezɛtsʊŋ] *n*
the argument

Das ist eine Auseinandersetzung
unter Männern.

This is an argument between men.

Möchten Sie ...?
['mœçtən zi: ...|] *phrase*
Would you like to...?

**Wie geht es Ihnen?;
Wie geht es dir?**
[vi: ge:t ɛs i:nən],
[vi: 'ge:t ɛs di:ɐ] *phrase*
How are you ?

Danke, gut
['daŋkə, 'gu:t] *phrase*
Fine,
thank you.

Herein!
[hɛ'raɪn] *interj*
Come in!

Bedien dich!
[bə'di:n dɪç] *phrase*
Please, help yourself!

Ja, gern.
['ja: 'gɛrn] *phrase*
Yes, please.

Entschuldigung!
[ɛnt'ʃʊldɪgʊŋ] *phrase*
I'm sorry!

Was ist los?
['vas ɪst 'lo:s] *phrase*
What's the matter?

Wie geht's?
[vi: 'ge:ts] *phrase*
How are you doing?

Ich hoffe es.
ɪç ˈhɔfə ɛs *phrase*
I hope so.

Hoffentlich nicht.
[ˈhɔfəntlɪç ˈnɪçt] *phrase*
I hope not

Sie wünschen?
[ziː ˈvʏnʃən] *phrase*
Can I help you?

Alles klar.
[ˈaləs ˈklaːɐ] *phrase*
All right.

Hier, bitte schön.
[ˈhiːɐ, ˈbɪtə ʃøːn] *phrase*
Here you are.

Das ist mir egal.
[das ɪst miːɐ eˈɡaːl] *phrase*
I don't mind.

Das ist mir egal, ich wollte sowieso einen neuen Wagen kaufen.

I don't mind, I was going to buy a new car anyway.

Das macht nichts.
[das 'maxt nɪçts] *phrase*
That doesn't matter.

Das macht nichts, ich bin ja Rechtshänder.

It doesn't matter, I'm right-handed

Nehmen Sie bitte Platz.
['ne:mən zi: 'bɪtə 'plats] *phrase*
Have a seat, please.

Nehmen Sie bitte Platz, meine Frau kommt auch gleich.

Have a seat, please, my wife will be here any minute.

Könnten Sie ...?
['kœntən zi: ...] *phrase*
Could you...?

Könnten Sie vielleicht ein bisschen kräftiger schieben?

Could you try pushing a bit harder?

Vorsicht!
['fo:zɪçt] *phrase*
Look out

Vorsicht! Der Taucher hat eine Harpune.

Look out, the diver's got a harpoon.

Keine Sorge!
['kaɪnə 'zɔrgə] *phrase*
Don't worry!

Keine Sorge, ich bin erst zweimal runtergefallen.

Don't worry, I've only fallen off twice before

Würdest du bitte ...?
['vʏrdəst du: 'bɪtə ...] *phrase*
Would you please...?

Würdest du bitte das Fenster zumachen?

Would you please close the window?

Lasst uns ...
['last ʊns ...] *phrase*
Let's...

Lasst uns mit dem 2. Satz weitermachen.

Let's continue with the 2nd movement.

der **Staat**
[ʃtaːt] *n*
the state

Jeder Staat braucht seine eigene Flagge.

Every state needs its own flag.

der Ausländer, die Ausländerin
['auslɛndɐ], ['auslɛndərin] *n*
the foreigner

Ausländer auf der Suche nach wilden Tieren.

Foreigners looking for wild animals.

das Land
[lant] *n*
the land, the country

In diesem Land lebten schon vor über 1500 Jahren Menschen.

People already lived in this country more than 1,500 years ago.

international
[ɪntɛnatsjo'naːl] *adj*
international

Wir müssen Sie über eine internationale Verbindung umleiten.

We're going to have to re-route you on an international flight.

national, National-
[natsjo'naːl] *adj*
national

Wenn die Nationalelf spielt, kann ich sehr laut werden.

I can be very noisy when the national team is playing.

die Fahne
['faːnə] *n*
the flag

Die vielen kleinen Fahnen begrüßen flatternd die Gäste.

Guests are greeted by lots of little flags fluttering in the breeze.

die Grenze
['gʁɛntsə] *n*
the border

Gegen den Ansturm der Barbaren wurde eine Grenze errichtet.

A border was built to ward off the attacks of the barbarians.

die Nation
[na'tsjoːn] *n*
the nation

die Nationalität
[natsjonali'tɛːt] *n*
the nationality

ausländisch
['auslɛndɪʃ] *adj*
foreign

staatlich
['ʃtaːtlɪç] *adj*
state

die Regierung
[re'gi:rʊŋ] n

the government

Die Regierung hat enge Verbindungen zur Kirche.

The government has close links to the Church.

der Präsident, die Präsidentin
[prezi'dɛnt], [prezi'dɛntɪn] n

the president

Präsidenten mit versteinerter Miene.

Stony-faced presidents.

das Parlament
[parla'mɛnt] n

the parliament

Das Parlament war bei der Abstimmung nicht vollzählig.

Not every member of parliament turned out for the vote.

die Opposition
[ɔpozi'tsjo:n] n

the opposition

Die Opposition bleibt standhaft!

The opposition is refusing to budge!

demokratisch
[demo'kra:tɪʃ] adj

democratic

Lassen Sie uns das auf demokratische Weise entscheiden.

Let's decide in a democratic manner.

Head of government in Germany and Austria is the Bundeskanzler (Federal Chancellor). The Bundespräsident (Federal President), officially head of state, has a more representative function.

der Minister, die Ministerin
[mi'nɪste], [mi'nɪstərɪn] n

the minister

45 Jahre in der Politik und erst jetzt endlich Minister.

A minister at last, after 45 years in politics.

die **Partei**
[par'taɪ] *n*
the party

Die Partei feierte eine
rauschende Party.

*The party threw
a massive party.*

die **Macht**
[maxt] *n*
the power, the force

Auch ohne sein Lichtschwert übt
er große Macht aus.

*He still wields great power, even
without his lightsabre.*

die **Politik**
[poli'tiːk] *n*
politics

Von Politik hab ich keine
Ahnung.

*I haven't got a clue about
politics.*

die **Botschaft**
['boːtʃaft] *n*
the embassy

Die Botschaft heißt ihre
Besucher willkommen.

*The embassy welcomes
visitors.*

regieren
[re'giːrən] *v*
to govern

herrschen
['hɛrʃən] *v*
to rule, to
reign

die
Demokratie
[demokra'tiː] *n*
the democracy

mächtig
['mɛçtɪç] *adj*
powerful

der/die
Abgeordnete
['apgəʔɔrdnətə] *n*
the Member
of Parliament

politisch
[po'liːtɪʃ] *adj*
political

das
Konsulat
[kɔnzu'laːt] *n*
the
consulate

die
Bevölkerung
[bə'fœlkərʊŋ] *n*
the
population

unterdrücken
[ʊntɐˈdrʏkən] *v*
to suppress

Sie versuchte vergeblich, das Niesen zu unterdrücken.

She tried in vain to suppress the sneeze.

der Diktator
[dɪkˈtaːtoːɐ] *n*
the dictator

Dieser Diktator ist ein Witz.

This dictator is a joke..

beeinflussen
[bəˈʔaɪnflʊsən] *v*
to influence

Herr Dr. Schmidt weiß, wie man Entscheidungen beeinflusst.

Dr Schmidt knows how to influence decisions.

unterschreiben
[ʊntɐˈʃraɪbən] *v*
to sign

Sie achtete überhaupt nicht darauf, was sie unterschrieb.

She didn't even look at what she was signing.

das Formular
[fɔrmuˈlaːɐ] *n*
the form

Vor der Behandlung müssen Sie erst alle Formulare ausfüllen.

You have to fill all the forms out before you receive treatment.

amtlich, offiziell
[ˈamtlɪç], [ɔfiˈtsjɛl] *adj*
official

Jetzt ist es amtlich: Die Krankenschwester erbt alles.

It's official now. The nurse inherits everything

die Verwaltung
[fɛɐˈvaltʊŋ] *n*
the administration

Die Verwaltung muss deutlich effizienter werden.

The administration needs to be much more efficient.

die **Krone**
['kro:nə] *n*
the **crown**

Diese Krone ist zu groß für Sie, Herr Vorsitzender.

This crown is too big for you, Your Honour.

die **Königin**
['kø:nɪgɪn] *n*
the **queen**

Die Königin war sehr erfreut.

The queen was very amused.

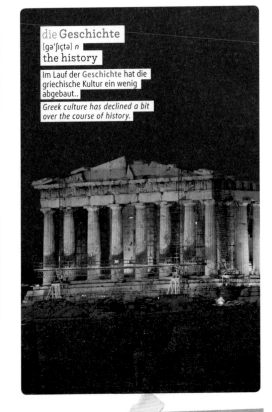

die **Geschichte**
[gə'ʃɪçtə] *n*
the **history**

Im Lauf der Geschichte hat die griechische Kultur ein wenig abgebaut..

Greek culture has declined a bit over the course of history.

der **König**
['kø:nɪç] *n*
the **king**

Die Könige glaubten schon, sich verirrt zu haben.

The kings thought they must have come to the wrong place.

sicher
['zɪçɐ] *adj*
safe

Dein Geld ist bei mir sicher.

Your money is safe with me.

der **Kaiser**
['kaize] *n*
the **emperor**

die **Kaiserin**
['kaɪzərɪn] *n*
the **empress**

die **Monarchie**
[monar'çi:] *n*
the **monarchy**

das **Königreich**
['kø:nɪgraɪç] *n*
the **kingdom**

Ich fühle mich wie Cäsar, nachdem er Gallien erobert hatte.

erobern
[εɐ'|oːbɛn] *v*
to conquer

I feel like Caesar when he conquered the Gauls.

der Krieg
[kriːk] *n*
the war

der Soldat, die Soldatin
[zɔl'daːt], [zɔl'daːtɪn] *n*
the soldier

die Armee
[ar'meː] *n*
the army

Eine Armee aus Terrakotta bewachte das Grab des Kaisers.

A terracotta army guarded the emperor's grave.

die Marine
[ma'riːnə] *n*
the navy

Die Marine der Schweiz hat jetzt auch ein U-Boot.

The Swiss navy now has its very own submarine.

die Luftwaffe
['lʊftvafə] *n*
the air force

Die Luftwaffe freut sich über jeden neuen Bewerber.

The air force welcomes all new applicants.

der Feind, die Feindin
[faɪnt], ['faɪndɪn] *n*
the enemy

Für manchen Sportler wird der Gegner zum Feind.

For some sportsmen, their opponents become their enemies.

kämpfen
['kɛmpfən] *v*
to fight

Hört sofort auf zu kämpfen!

Stop fighting at once!!

der Konflikt
[kɔn'flɪkt] *n*
the conflict

Solange keiner nachgibt, bleibt der Konflikt unlösbar.

It will be impossible to solve the conflict if nobody budges.

der Terrorist, die Terroristin
[tɛro'rɪst], [tɛro'rɪstɪn] *n*
the terrorist

Sie behandeln mich, als wäre ich eine Terroristin!

You're treating me as if I was a terrorist!

bewaffnet
[bə'vafnət] *adj*
armed

Vorsicht, er ist bewaffnet!

Be careful, he's armed!

die Waffe
['vafə] *n*
the weapon

David interessierte sich schon als kleiner Junge für Waffen.

David was interested in weapons from when he was a small boy.

schießen
['ʃiːsən] *v*
to shoot

Wenn ich schieße, lachen sich die Enten tot.

When I shoot, the ducks die of laughter.

friedlich
['friːtlɪç] *adj*
peaceful

Solange ich ihr meine Gitarre ließ, blieb sie friedlich.

She stayed peaceful as long as I let her have my guitar.

der Frieden
['friːdən] *n*
the peace

Man muss den Frieden festhalten – mit aller Gewalt.

We need to hold onto peace – as forcefully as possible.

SOCIETY & THE LAW

die **Gesellschaft**
[gəˈzɛlʃaft] *n*
the society

Du musst deinen Platz in der **Gesellschaft** finden – ganz ohne GPS und Navi.

You need to find your own place in society – without any satnavs or GPS devices.

die Öffentlichkeit
['œfantlɪçkaɪt] n
the public

Wer in der Öffentlichkeit steht, muss mit Beobachtung rechnen.

If you're in the public eye, you should expect to be watched.

privat, Privat-
[pri'vaːt] adj
private

Im Privatjet fliegt sich's einfach am angenehmsten.

Flying is so much more fun in a private jet.

arm
['aʀm] adj
poor

Wer arm ist, kann trotzdem seine Würde bewahren.

Being poor doesn't mean you can't keep your dignity.

reich
[ʀaɪç] adj
rich

Wir sind reich, wir sind schön – sonst noch Fragen?

We're rich, we're beautiful – anything else you need to know?

der Mangel
['maŋəl] n
the lack

In einem Privatjet hätte ich jetzt keinen Platzmangel.

There would be no lack of legroom if I was in a private jet.

das Elend
['eːlɛnt] n
the misery

Das Elend dieses armen Hundes mag man sich kaum vorstellen.

We can only imagine the misery the poor dog felt.

öffentlich
['œfantlɪç] adj
public

sozial, gesellschaftlich
[zo'tsiaːl], [gə'zɛlʃaftlɪç] adj
social

der Reichtum
['ʀaɪçtuːm] n
the wealth

die Armut
['armuːt] n
the poverty

die **Religion**
[reli'gio:n] *n*
the religion

Religion ist der Glaube an eine Macht, die über dem Menschen steht.

Religion is the belief in a higher power.

der **Gott**
[gɔt] *n*
the god

Ägyptens Herrscher wurden auch als Götter verehrt.

Egypt's rulers were also revered as gods.

The plural of Gott is Götter (gods), the feminine form is Göttin (goddess).

beten
['be:tən] *v*
to pray

Sag nichts, bis er mit dem Beten fertig ist.

Don't say anything until he's finished praying.

der **Glaube**
['glaubə] *n*
the faith

Ihr Glaube hat sie bis nach Mekka gebracht.

Their faith has got them here to Mekka.

die **Freiheit**
['fraɪhaɪt] n
the freedom

Freiheit kann auch ganz
schön anstrengend sein.

*Freedom can also be
quite hard work.*

der **Atheist**,
die **Atheistin**
[ate'ɪst], [ate'ɪstɪn] n
the atheist

Ist dieser Mann wirklich
ein **Atheist**?

Is this man really an atheist?

die **Gerechtigkeit**
[gə'rɛçtɪçkaɪt] n
the justice

Die **Gerechtigkeit** ist blind, aber
sie lässt sich gerne vergolden.

*Justice is blind, but it doesn't
mind being gilded.*

unschuldig
['ʊnʃʊldɪç] adj
innocent

So **unschuldig** sieht Jan nur
aus, wenn er schläft.

*Jan only looks this innocent
when he's asleep.*

schuldig
['ʃʊldɪç] adj
guilty

Nicht jeder, der im Gefängnis
sitzt, muss auch **schuldig** sein.

*Not everyone in jail is
necessarily guilty.*

moralisch
[mo'ra:lɪʃ] adj
moral

Ich habe geschworen, ein
moralisches Leben zu führen.

*I have sworn to live
a moral life.*

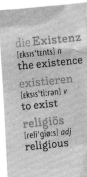

die **Existenz**
[ɛksɪs'tɛnts] n
the existence

existieren
[ɛksɪs'ti:rən] v
to exist

religiös
[reli'giø:s] adj
religious

die **Schuld**
[ʃʊlt] n
the guilt

frei
[fraɪ] adj
free

unmoralisch
['ʊnmoralɪʃ] adj
immoral

gerecht
[gə'rɛçt] adj
just

ungerecht
['ʊngərɛçt] adj
unjust

das Gesetz
[gə'zɛts] n
the law

Echt? Sie haben alle diese Gesetze auswendig gelernt?

Seriously? You learned all these laws off by heart?

das Recht
[rɛçt] n
the right

Meinungsfreiheit gehört zu den grundlegenden Menschenrechten.

Freedom of speech is a basic human right.

legal
[le'gaːl] adj
legal

Glaubst du wirklich, dass Sprayen hier legal ist?

Do you really think spray painting graffiti is legal here?

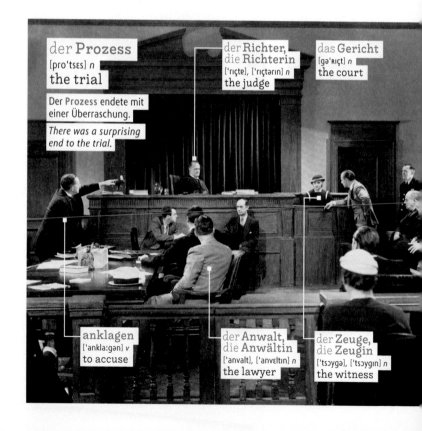

der Prozess
[pro'tsɛs] n
the trial

Der Prozess endete mit einer Überraschung.

There was a surprising end to the trial.

der Richter, die Richterin
['rɪçtɐ], ['rɪçtərɪn] n
the judge

das Gericht
[gə'rɪçt] n
the court

anklagen
['anklaːgən] v
to accuse

der Anwalt, die Anwältin
['anvalt], ['anvɛltɪn] n
the lawyer

der Zeuge, die Zeugin
['tsɔygə], ['tsɔygɪn] n
the witness

das **Opfer**
[ˈɔpfɐ] *n*
the victim

Nie wieder Opfer! Morgen gehe
ich zum Taekwondo..

*No more being the victim! I'm
starting taekwondo tomorrow*

das **Verbrechen**
[fɛɐ̯ˈbrɛçən] *n*
the crime

Verbrechen ist unser Geschäft.

Crime is our business.

stehlen
[ˈʃteːlən] *v*
to steal

Was heißt hier stehlen?
Wir haben Hunger!

*What do you mean
stealing? We're hungry!*

die **Strafe**
[ˈʃtraːfə] *n*
the punishment

Ben fand seine Strafe furchtbar
ungerecht.

*Ben thought his punishment
terribly unfair.*

töten, umbringen
[ˈtøːtən], [ˈʊmbrɪŋən] *v*
to kill

Schau mal, Erika: Diese Mücke
habe ich selbst getötet.

*Erika, look, I killed this
mosquito all by myself.*

der **Diebstahl**
[ˈdiːpʃtaːl] *n*
the theft

der/die **Angeklagte**
[ˈangəklaːktə] *n*
the accused

der **Mord**
[mɔrt] *n*
the murder

illegal
[ˈɪlegaːl] *adj*
illegal

die **Industrie**
[ɪndʊ'striː] *n*
the industry

In der Industrie sind die
Arbeitsplätze rar geworden.

*Jobs in industry have
become scarce.*

die **Firma**
['fɪrma] *n*
the firm,
the company

Wir sind zwar klein, aber schon eine richtige **Firma**.

We may be small, but we're still a proper company.

die **Wirtschaft**
['vɪrtʃaft] *n*
the economy

Mit der **Wirtschaft** geht es ständig auf und ab.

The economy is up and down like a yo-yo.

die **Bank**
[baŋk] *n*
the bank

Die **Banken** haben in London ein eigenes Viertel.

In London, the banks have their own district.

sparen
['ʃpaːrən] *v*
to save

Auf einem Sparbuch zu sparen kann ich mir **sparen**.

I like to save myself the bother of a savings account.

wechseln
['vɛksəln] *v*
wechseln

Das kann doch nicht so schwer sein: Ich würde gern alle meine Münzen in Scheine **wechseln**.

How hard can it be? I just want to change all my coins into notes.

die **Ware**
['vaːrə] *n*
the merchandise,
the goods

Das große Angebot an **Waren** überfordert mich.

I find the huge range of goods overwhelming.

die **Aktiengesellschaft**
['aktsiəngəzelʃaft] *n*
the public limited company,
the corporation

die **Nachfrage**
['naːxfraːgə] *n*
the demand

der **Umsatz**
['ʊmzats] *n*
the turnover

die Versicherung
[fɛɐˈzɪçərʊŋ] *n*
the insurance

Ich kann nur hoffen, dass die Versicherung zahlt.

I'll just have to hope that the insurance pays out.

die Schulden
[ˈʃʊldən] *n*
the debts

Frau und Hund auf und davon, geblieben sind nur die Schulden.

The wife and the dog have upped and left and all that's left are the debts.

das Kleingeld
[ˈklaɪnɡɛlt] *n*
the change

Vielen Dank, das Kleingeld kann ich gut gebrauchen.

Thanks, the change will come in very handy.

das Geld
[ɡɛlt] *n*
the money

Ich finde Geld total unwichtig – solange ich eine Kreditkarte habe.

Money doesn't matter to me at all – as long as I have a credit card.

die Kreditkarte
[kreˈdiːtkartə] *n*
the credit card

die Münze
[ˈmʏntsə] *n*
the coin

die Banknote
[ˈbaŋknoːtə] *n*
the banknote

der Cent
[sɛnt] *n*
the cent

der Euro
[ˈɔyro] *n*
the euro

erhöhen, steigern
[ɛɛˈhøːən], [ˈʃtaɪɡən] *v*
to increase

Wir müssen die Geschwindigkeit erhöhen, sonst hängen wir hier fest.

We need to increase our speed or we'll get stuck here.

sich lohnen
[zɪç ˈloːnən] *v*
to be worthwhile

Hier lohnt sich eine Reparatur nicht mehr.

It's not worthwhile repairing this lot anymore.

importieren
[ɪmpɔrˈtiːrən] *v*
to import

All diese Früchte sind importiert.

All these fruits are imported.

die Bestellung
[bəˈʃtɛlʊŋ] *n*
the order

Die Bestellung beim schwerhörigen Kellner wurde kompliziert.

Giving our order to the hard-of-hearing waiter was quite tricky.

verringern, senken
[fɛɛˈrɪŋən], [ˈzɛŋkən] *v*
to reduce

Urplötzlich verringerte Graf Wumme sein Tempo.

All of a sudden, Count Wumme reduced his speed.

sinken, sich verringern
[ˈzɪŋkən], [zɪç fɛɛˈrɪŋən] *v*
to decrease

schulden
[ˈʃʊldən] *v*
to owe

exportieren
[ɛkspɔrˈtiːrən] *v*
to export

versichern
[fɛɛˈzɪçən] *v*
to insure

die **Landwirtschaft**
['lantvɪrtʃaft] *n*
the agriculture

So kann ich Landwirtschaft und Fliegen miteinander verbinden.

This way, I get to combine agriculture and flying.

pflanzen
['pflantsən] *v*
to plant

Gestern gepflanzt, heute gegossen – wo bleiben die Tomaten?

I planted them yesterday and watered them today, so where are the tomatoes?

fruchtbar
['frʊxtba:e] *adj*
fertile

Wenn nur mein Pandabär auch so fruchtbar wäre!

I just wish my panda was that fertile!

landwirt-schaftlich
['lantvɪrtʃaftlɪç] *adj*
agricultural

ernten
['ɛrntən] *v*
to harvest

die **Methode**
[me'to:də] *n*
the method

die **Ernte**
['ɛrntə] *n*
the harvest

Die Ernte war dieses Jahr besonders ertragreich. Der Lohn dagegen weniger.

The harvest was particularly good this year, unlike the wages.

anbauen
['anbauən] *v*
to grow

Unsere Familie baut seit drei Generationen Reis an.

Our family has been growing rice for three generations.

die **Art und Weise**
[aːet ʊnt 'vaɪzə] *n*
the way

Deine Art und Weise, Dame zu spielen, nervt mich kolossal.

I find your way of playing draughts incredibly annoying.

der **Bauernhof**
['bauernhoːf] *n*
the farm

Gleich hinter den Feldern lag ein Bauernhof.

There was a farm right behind the fields.

das **Feld**
[fɛlt] *n*
the field

wie
[viː] *conj*
how

Weißt du wirklich, wie man das repariert?

Do you really know how to repair it?

die Maschine, das Gerät
['maʃiːnə] [gəˈrɛːt] *n*
the machine

Die Maschine, die unser Leben wirklich verändert hat, ist die Waschmaschine.

The machine that has really changed our lives is the washing machine.

funktionieren
[fʊŋktsjoˈniːʀən] *v*
to work

Glaubst du wirklich, die funktionieren noch, Bärchen?

Do you really think they still work, sweetie?

elektrisch
[eˈlɛktrɪʃ] *adj*
electric

Ich benutze jetzt nur noch deine elektrische Zahnbürste, Papa.

From now on I'll only be using your electric toothbrush, Daddy.

der Motor
['moːtoːɐ] *n*
the motor, the engine

Elektromotoren treiben die Fertigungsstraße der Automotoren an.

The car engine production line is driven by electric motors.

erfinden
[ɛɐ̯'fɪndən] *v*
to invent

Ich habe ein Gerät erfunden, das ihre Gedanken lesen kann.

I've invented a machine that can read her mind.

entdecken
[ɛnt'dɛkən] *v*
to discover

Houston? Ich glaube, ich habe hier Fußspuren entdeckt …

Houston? Ich glaube, ich habe hier Fußspuren entdeckt …

die Kraft
[kraft] *n*
the power

Der Damm erzeugt Strom aus der Kraft des Wassers.

The dam generates hydroelectric power.

die Energie
[enɐr'giː] *n*
the energy

Wenn Wind weht, wird die Stadt mit Energie versorgt.

If it's windy, the city is supplied with energy.

das System
[zʏs'teːm] *n*
the system

Ein gutes System kann man erweitern.

A good system is expandable.

bauen
['bauən] *v*
to build

Ich baue hier für die Ewigkeit.

This is built to last.

die Elektrizität
[elɛktritsi'tɛːt] *n*
the electricity

die Entdeckung
[ɛnt'dɛkʊŋ] *n*
the discovery

die Erfindung
[ɛɐ̯'fɪndʊŋ] *n*
the invention

die Funktion
[fʊŋk'tsjoːn] *n*
the function

das Material
[mate'ria:l] *n*
the material

Es gibt keinen Abfall, nur Material für Möglichkeiten.

There's such thing as waste, just material for new opportunities.

das Glas
[gla:s] *n*
the glass

der Kunststoff, das Plastik
['kʊnstʃtɔf], [plastɪk] *n*
the plastic

reparieren
[ʀepa'ʀi:ʀən] *v*
to repair

Wie lange man Autos wohl noch selbst reparieren kann?

How much longer will people still be able to repair cars themselves?

genau
[gə'nau] *adv*
precisely

Gleich sage ich dir, wie spät es genau ist.

Give me a second and I'll be able to tell you precisely what time it is.

dünn
[dʏn] *adj*
thin

dick
[dɪk] *adj*
thick

Meine Güte, entscheide dich: das dicke oder das dünne Seil?

Come on, make your mind up – do you want the thick rope or the thin one?

weich
[vaɪç] *adj*
soft

Sooo weich ist nur mein Teddybär.

Nothing's as soft as my teddy bear.

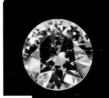

hart
[haʁt] *adv*
hard

Ich habe für die Verlobung hart gearbeitet.

I've worked hard for the engagement.

zerbrechlich
[tsɛɐ'bʁɛçlɪç] *adj*
fragile

Na sowas! Die sind zerbrechlich.

Gee! They're fragile!

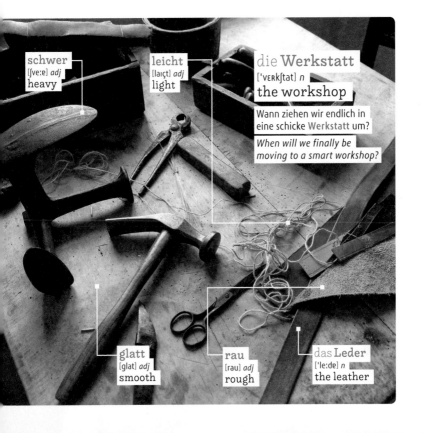

schwer
[ʃveːɐ] *adj*
heavy

leicht
[laɪçt] *adj*
light

die **Werkstatt**
['vɛʁkʃtat] *n*
the workshop

Wann ziehen wir endlich in eine schicke Werkstatt um?

When will we finally be moving to a smart workshop?

glatt
[glat] *adj*
smooth

rau
[rau] *adj*
rough

das **Leder**
['leːdɐ] *n*
the leather

das Leben

['le:bən] *n*
the life

Wo das Leben pulsiert, kommt man sich zwangsweise näher.

In a place thronging with life, you can't help getting closer to each other.

EVERY-
DAY
LIFE

das **Haus**
[haus] *n*

the house

Die Leiter zum **Haus** ist gegen einen geringen Aufpreis erhältlich.

The ladder for the house is available at a small extra charge.

Words for different types of house include *Reihenhaus* (terraced house), *Hochhaus* (high rise) or *Wolkenkratzer* (skyscraper) and *Einfamilienhaus* (single-familiy house).

die **Adresse**
[aˈdrɛsə] *n*
the address

Zu dieser Adresse bring ich keine Briefe mehr.

I'm not delivering any letters to this address anymore.

der **Wohnort**
[ˈvoːnˌɔrt] *n*
the (place of) residence

Wie gefällt dir die Aussicht an meinem neuen Wohnort?

How do you like the view from my new residence?

die **Hausnummer**
[ˈhausnʊmɐ] *n*
the house number

Kannst du dich an Maggies Hausnummer erinnern?

Can you remember Maggie's house number?

zu **Hause**
[tsu: ˈhauzə] *adv*
at home

Nur wenn die Katze im Haus ist, fühle ich mich zu Hause.

I only feel truly at home when the cat's in the house.

die **Etage**
[eˈtaːʒə] *n*
the floor

Ich glaube, es war die fünfte Etage, aber es gibt hier ja so viel Auswahl.

I think it was the fifth floor, but there are so many to choose from.

das **Erdgeschoss**
[ˈeːɐtɡəʃɔs] *n*
the ground floor

Wir leben im Erdgeschoss, damit Chrissi jederzeit raus kann.

We live on the ground floor so Chrissi can go out whenever she likes.

kommen aus/von
[ˈkɔmən ˈaus/ˈfɔn] *v*
to be from, to come from

Ich komme vom Planeten XQ6TL-038P#

I'm from planet XQ6TL-038P#.

der **Eingang**
['aɪŋɡaŋ] *n*
the entrance

der **Ausgang**
['ausɡaŋ] *n*
the exit

Eine Drehtür ist Eingang und Ausgang zugleich.

A revolving door is both an entrance and an exit at the same time.

die **Tür**
['ty:ɐ] *n*
the door

Nur bei Vollmond ist jene Tür sichtbar.

You can only see that door by the light of a full moon.

mieten
['mi:tən] *v*
to hire, to rent

Die Hell's Angels haben heute diese Fahrräder gemietet. Das darf aber keiner wissen.

Don't tell anyone, but the Hell's Angels have hired these bikes today.

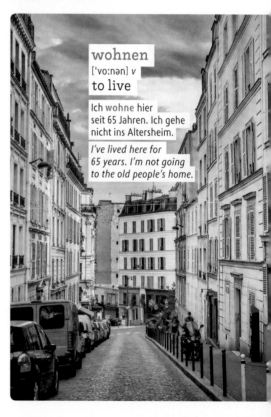

wohnen
['vo:nən] *v*
to live

Ich wohne hier seit 65 Jahren. Ich gehe nicht ins Altersheim.

I've lived here for 65 years. I'm not going to the old people's home.

vermieten
[fɛɐ'mi:tən] *v*
to let

Ich vermiete mein Sofa an Touristen.

I let my sofa to tourists.

das Tor
['to:e] *n*
the gate

Dieses Tor soll nie wieder
geschlossen werden.

*This gate must never be closed
again.*

das Dach
[dax] *n*
the roof

Zumindest haben sie ein Dach
über dem Kopf.

*At least they have a roof over
their heads.*

der Aufzug
['auftsu:k] *n*
the lift,
the elevator

Lass uns die Treppe
nehmen, der Aufzug
ist mir zu teuer.

*Let's use the stairs, the
lift's too expensive for me.*

das Zimmer,
der Raum
['tsɪmɐ], [raum] *n*
the room

Sag mal, musst du das Rad immer
mit aufs Zimmer nehmen?

*Do you really always have to take
your bike into your room with you?*

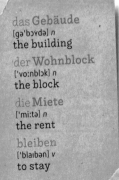

das Gebäude
[gə'bɔʏdə] *n*
the building

der Wohnblock
['vo:nblɔk] *n*
the block

die Miete
['mi:tə] *n*
the rent

bleiben
['blaɪbən] *v*
to stay

klingeln
['klɪŋəln] *v*
to ring the bell

Klingeln Sie, Herr Kommissar, ich hole schon mal den Wagen.

You ring the bell, inspector, while I get the car.

öffnen, aufmachen
['œfnən], ['aufmaxən] *v*
to open

Frauchen, mach doch mal die Falle auf.

Go on, Mum, open the trap.

schließen, zumachen
['ʃliːsən], ['tsuːmaxən] *v*
to shut, to close

Schließ die Augen und entspann' dich.

Just close your eyes and relax.

die Decke
['dɛkə] *n*
the ceiling

Die Decke lebt. Bald kommt sie runter.

The ceiling's alive. It'll be coming down soon

das Fenster
['fɛnstɐ] *n*
the window

Als Abteilungsleiter habe ich endlich ein Büro mit Fenster.

Now that I'm head of department I finally get an office with a window.

die Wand, die Mauer
[vant], ['maue] *n*
the wall

Die Kinder sind an die Wand gemalt, die Schaukel ist echt.

The children are painted on the wall, but the swing's real.

der (Fuß)Boden
['(fuːs)boːdən] *n*
the floor

Morgens muss ich erst testen, wie kalt der Fußboden ist.

In the mornings, I have to test the floor to see how cold it is.

die **Terrasse**
[tɛˈrasə] *n*
the terrace

Mia hatte es sich mit ihrem Donut auf der Terrasse gemütlich gemacht.

Mia had settled down comfortably on the terrace with her doughnut.

der **Balkon**
[ˈbælkən] *n*
the balcony

Kommst du heute Nacht zu mir auf den Balkon?

Will you come out onto the balcony to see me tonight?

die **Treppe**
[ˈtrɛpə] *n*
the stairs

Auf dieser Treppe wird mir immer schwindelig.

I always get dizzy on these stairs.

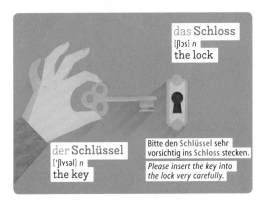

das **Schloss**
[ʃlɔs] *n*
the lock

der **Schlüssel**
[ˈʃlʏsəl] *n*
the key

Bitte den Schlüssel sehr vorsichtig ins Schloss stecken.

Please insert the key into the lock very carefully.

der **Keller**
[ˈkɛlɐ] *n*
the cellar

Theo hat ein paar echte Schätzchen im Keller.

Theo has a couple of real beauties in the cellar.

die **Garage**
[gaˈraːʒə] *n*
the garage

Von der Garage zum Einsatzort brauchten sie nur drei Minuten.

It only took them three minutes to get from the garage to the scene.

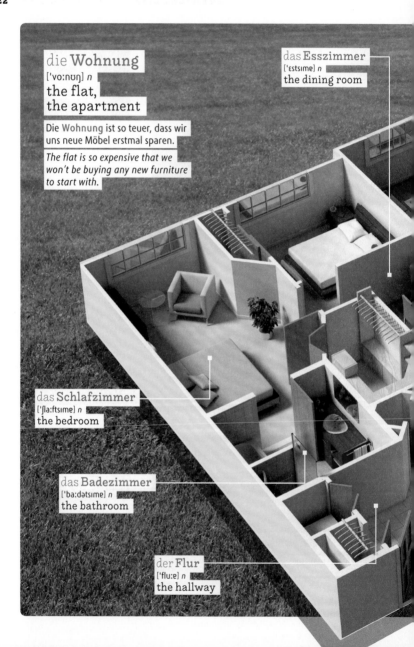

die Wohnung
['voːnʊŋ] *n*
the flat,
the apartment

Die Wohnung ist so teuer, dass wir uns neue Möbel erstmal sparen.

The flat is so expensive that we won't be buying any new furniture to start with.

das Esszimmer
['ɛstsɪme] *n*
the dining room

das Schlafzimmer
['ʃlaːftsɪme] *n*
the bedroom

das Badezimmer
['baːdətsɪme] *n*
the bathroom

der Flur
['fluːe] *n*
the hallway

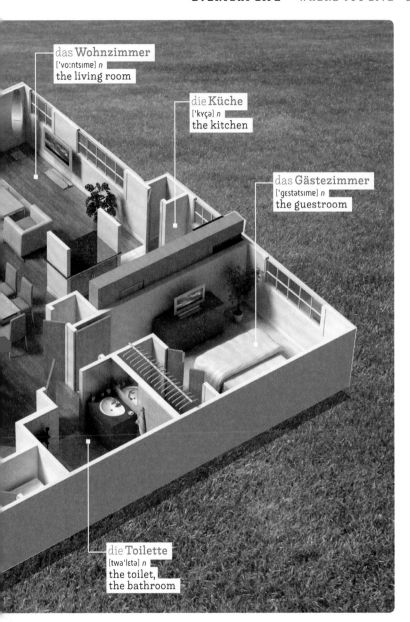

das **Wohnzimmer**
[ˈvoːntsɪmɐ] *n*
the living room

die **Küche**
[ˈkʏçə] *n*
the kitchen

das **Gästezimmer**
[ˈgɛstətsɪmɐ] *n*
the guestroom

die **Toilette**
[twaˈlɛtə] *n*
the toilet,
the bathroom

die Dusche
['du:ʃə] *n*
the shower

Dusche oder Badewanne?
Sauber wird man in jedem Fall.

*Shower or bath? I'll come
out clean either way.*

die Badewanne
['ba:dəvanə] *n*
the bath(tub)

die Zahnbürste
['tsa:nbʏrstə] *n*
the toothbrush

Die Zahnbürste war ein sicheres
Zeichen: Sie würde bleiben.

*The toothbrush was a sure sign
that she would stay.*

das Handtuch
['hanttu:x] *n*
the towel

Ein Handtuch zum
Reservieren der Liege
reicht nicht mehr.

*It's no longer enough just
to put a towel down
to reserve your deckchair.*

sich rasieren
[zɪç ra'zi:rən] *v*
to shave

Lass den Quatsch, Papa, ich
muss mich noch nicht rasieren.

*Don't be silly, Daddy, I'm not
old enough to start shaving yet.*

Zähne putzen
['tsɛ:nə pʊtsən] *phrase*
to brush one's teeth

Wenn ich mir morgens die **Zähne
putze**, schlafe ich meistens noch.

*I'm normally still half-asleep
when I brush my teeth in the
morning.*

duschen
['du:ʃən] *v*
to have a shower

Warum mit Getier im Meer baden, wenn ich am Strand auch duschen kann?

Why would I want to swim with all those creatures in the sea when I can just as well have a shower on the beach?

baden
['ba:dən] *v*
to have a bath

Wenn Henry badet, singt er am liebsten ABBA.

Henry likes singing ABBA songs when he has a bath.

der Kamm
[kam] *n*
the comb

Ich habe mir für meinen Bart extra einen Kamm zugelegt.

I got a special comb for my beard.

das Shampoo
['ʃampu:] *n*
the shampoo

Dieses Shampoo schäumt einfach ohne Ende.

This shampoo is incredibly foamy.

der Föhn
[fø:n] *n*
the hairdryer

Dass ein einfacher Föhn solche Gefühle wecken kann …

You wouldn't think that a humble hairdryer could awaken such feelings …

die Haarbürste
['ha:ebʏrstə] *n*
the hairbrush

die Seife
['zaifə] *n*
the soap

die Creme
[kre:m] *n*
the cream

die Zahnpasta
['tsa:npasta] *n*
the toothpaste

HOME COMFORTS

die **Möbel**
['møːbəl] *n*
the furniture

Überraschung, mein Bärchen:
Wir richten uns komplett
neu ein – und diese alten Möbel
kommen auf den Sperrmüll.

Surprise, honey: we're
giving the place a complete
makeover – and all this old
furniture is going to the dump.

der **Tisch**
[tɪʃ] *n*
the table

der **Stuhl**
[ʃtuːl] *n*
the chair

der Schrank
[ʃraŋk] *n*
the cupboard

Hörst du auch diese komischen Geräusche aus dem Schrank?

Can you hear those funny noises in the cupboard, too?

die Lampe
['lampə] *n*
the lamp

Bah, mit einer Lampe, die nur raucht, kann ich nichts anfangen.

Hah, what use is a smoking lamp to me?

das Bett
[bɛt] *n*
the bed

Bei Mama im Bett ist es sonntags einfach am schönsten.

Nothing beats being in bed with Mummy on a Sunday.

sitzen
['zɪtsən] *v*
to sit

Ich fand es leicht unheimlich, wie die Katze dort saß und mich anblickte.

I found the way the cat just sat there and stared at me a bit unnerving.

bequem
[bə'kveːm] *adj*
comfortable

Ohne diese Schuhe ist es so viel bequemer.

It's much more comfortable without these shoes.

einschalten, anmachen
['aɪnʃaltən], ['anmaxən] *v*
to turn on

ausschalten, ausmachen
['ausʃaltən], ['ausmaxən] *v*
to turn off

Einschalten und ausschalten ist hier gar nicht so einfach.

Turning it on and off isn't so easy here.

heizen
['haɪtsən] *v*
to heat

Für meine Katze muss ich immer extra heizen.

I always have to heat the house specially for my cat.

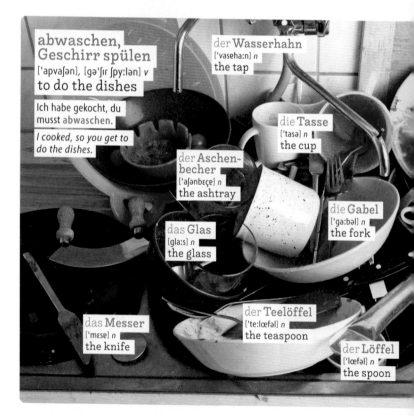

abwaschen, Geschirr spülen
['apvaʃən], [gə'ʃɪr ʃpy:lən] *v*
to do the dishes

Ich habe gekocht, du musst abwaschen.

I cooked, so you get to do the dishes.

der **Wasserhahn**
['vaseha:n] *n*
the tap

die **Tasse**
['tasə] *n*
the cup

der **Aschen-becher**
['aʃənbɛçɐ] *n*
the ashtray

das **Glas**
[gla:s] *n*
the glass

die **Gabel**
['ga:bəl] *n*
the fork

das **Messer**
['mɛsɐ] *n*
the knife

der **Teelöffel**
['te:lœfəl] *n*
the teaspoon

der **Löffel**
['lœfəl] *n*
the spoon

die Heizung
[ˈhaɪtsʊŋ] *n*
the heating

Die Zentralheizung des ganzen Sonnensystems.

The central heating for the entire solar system.

der Teller
[ˈtɛlɐ] *n*
the plate

die Pfanne
[ˈpfanə] *n*
the frying pan

Schon gut, Mama, ich hol' mir die Milch selbst aus dem Kühlschrank!

der Kühlschrank
[ˈkyːlʃraŋk] *n*
the fridge

Don't worry, Mummy, I'll get the milk out of the fridge myself!

der Herd
[ˈheːɐt] *n*
the cooker, the stove

Zu Hause hab' ich natürlich einen Induktionsherd.

Of course, I've got an induction cooker at home.

der Kochtopf
[ˈkɔxtɔpf] *n*
the pot

Wir haben nur einen Kochtopf, da muss eben alles rein.

We've only got the one pot, so it all has to go in there together.

die Schachtel
['ʃaxtəl] n
the box

Maria will gar nicht mehr raus aus ihrer Schachtel.

Maria doesn't want to come out of her box.

der Spiegel
['ʃpiːgəl] n
the mirror

Er konnte sich stundenlang im Spiegel betrachten.

He could spend hours looking at himself in the mirror.

die Wasch-maschine
['vaʃmaʃiːnə] n
the washing machine

Meine Waschmaschine frisst meine Socken.

My washing machine eats my socks.

die Kerze
['kɛrtsə] n
the candle

anzünden
['antsʏndən] v
to light

Jede Kerze, die wir anzünden, ist mit dem Gedanken an einen lieben Menschen verbunden.

Every candle we light is to remind us of someone we love.

die **Mülltonne**
['mʏltɔnə] *n*
the rubbish bin

Erstaunlich, was man so alles in der Mülltonne findet.

It's amazing what you find in the rubbish bin.

sauber
['zaubɐ] *adj*
clean

Absolut saubere Energie ist eine Illusion.

Totally clean energy is an illusion.

schmutzig
['ʃmʊtsɪç] *adj*
dirty

Ihr seid aber schmutzig! Na, dann gebt schnell noch dem Papa ein Küsschen.

Look how dirty you are! Never mind, give Daddy a quick kiss.

waschen
['vaʃən] *v*
to wash

Timmy hält waschen für überbewertet.

Timmy thinks washing is overrated.

trocknen
['trɔknən] *v*
to dry

Ich glaube, die Farbe deiner Hemden leidet, wenn wir sie im Garten trocknen.

I think the colour of your shirts suffers from drying them in the garden.

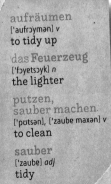

aufräumen
['aufrɔymən] *v*
to tidy up

das **Feuerzeug**
['fɔyɐtsɔyk] *n*
the lighter

**putzen,
sauber machen.**
['pʊtsən], ['zaubɐ maxən] *v*
to clean

sauber
['zaubɐ] *adj*
tidy

Wenn Sie glauben, dass irgendwelche Apps eine klassische Bildung ersetzen können, dann sind Sie auf dem Holzweg!

die **Bildung**
[ˈbɪldʊŋ] *n*
the education

If you think a few apps can replace a traditional education, you've got another thing coming!

lernen
['lɛrnən] *v*
to learn

Mit Ihnen lerne ich am liebsten, Herr Karloff.

I like learning with you best, Mr Karloff .

studieren
[ʃtu'diːrən] *v*
to study

Nur ausgeschlafen kann man gut studieren.

You can only study properly if you've had enough sleep.

das Wissen
['vɪsən] *n*
the knowledge

Mein ganzes Wissen stammt aus alten Büchern.

My knowledge all comes from old books.

wissen
['vɪsən] *v*
to know

Blöde Streber, wissen mal wieder alles.

Don't they just know it all, the little swots.

über, von
['yːbɐ], [fɔn] *prep*
about

Über diese Sache weiß ich absolut nichts.

I know absolutely nothing about it.

erklären
[ɛɐ'klɛːrən] *v*
to explain

verstehen
[fɛɐ'ʃteːən] *v*
to understand

Ich erkläre und erkläre, aber Opa versteht's einfach nicht.

However much I explain it, Granddad just doesn't seem to understand.

begreifen
[bə'graifən] *n*
to realize

die Erklärung
[ɛ'klɛːrʊŋ] *n*
the explanation; the declaration

hervorragend
[hɛr'foːɐragənd] *n*
brilliant

die Klasse
['klasə] *n*
the class

So schön ruhig war es in der Klasse schon lange nicht mehr.

It hasn't been this quiet in class for ages.

das Klassenzimmer
['klasəntsɪmɐ] *n*
the classroom

der Unterricht
['ʊntɐrɪçt] *n*
the teaching, the classes

unterrichten
[ʊntɐ'rɪçtən] *v*
to teach

Wenn ich unterrichte, werfe ich die Schüler ins kalte Wasser.

When I teach, I like to throw my pupils in at the deep end.

interessant
[ɪntaʀɛ'sant] *adj*
interesting

Das Kunstwerk war ... äh ... interessant.

The work of art was ... um ... interesting.

sich interessieren (für)
[zɪç ɪntaʀɛ'siːrən (fyːɐ)] *v*
to be interested (in)

Anna interessiert sich mehr für Simon, als ihm lieb ist.

Anna is more interested in Simon than he would like.

die Übung
['y:bʊŋ] n
the exercise

Diese Übung bitte dreimal täglich wiederholen.

Repeat this exercise three times a day.

der Schüler, die Schülerin
['ʃy:lɐ], ['ʃy:lərɪn] n
the pupil, the schoolboy, the schoolgirl

Es gibt Schüler, die gehen richtig gern zur Schule.

Some pupils really love going to school.

das Beispiel
['baɪʃpi:l] n
the example

Ein gutes Beispiel für Lehrmaterial im Biologieunterricht.

A good example of the teaching materials you can use for biology.

das Fach
[fax] n
the subject

Das Fach Chemie kann richtig Spaß machen.

Chemistry can be a really fun subject.

die Schule
['ʃu:lə] n
the school

In den Ferien ist die Schule gespenstisch.

The school is an eerie place during the holidays.

spicken, abschreiben
['ʃpɪkən], ['apʃraibən] v
to crib, to cheat

Einige der Schüler spickten während der Prüfung.

Some of the students were cheating during the exam.

der Lehrer, die Lehrerin
['le:rɐ], ['le:rərɪn] n
the teacher

das Interesse
[ɪntə'rɛsə] n
the interest

der Stundenplan
['ʃtʊndənpla:n] n
the timetable

der Kurs
['kʊʀs] n
the course

Sarah will im Kurs immer allen zeigen, dass sie die Beste ist.

Sarah always wants to show everyone else on the course that she's the best.

das Studium
['ʃtuːdiʊm] n
studies

Doch, glaub's mir ruhig, wir sind mitten im Studium.

Take my word for it, we're in the middle of our studies.

der Professor, die Professorin
[pro'fɛsoːɐ], [profɛ'soːrɪn] n
the professor

Unser Professor wäre so gerne berühmt.

Our professor wishes he was famous.

die Universität
[ʊniverzi'tɛːt] n
the university

Ich bin total neidisch: ich wünschte, unsere Universität hätte eine so schöne Bibliothek.

I'm so jealous, I wish our university had such a nice library.

der Student, die Studentin
[ʃtu'dɛnt], [ʃtu'dɛntɪn] n
the student (at a university or college)

abwesend, nicht da
['apve:zənt], [nɪçt 'da:] *adj*
absent

Valerie scheint heute nicht da zu sein …

Valerie seems to be absent today …

anwesend, da
['anve:zənt], [da:] *adj*
present

Moment, da sitzt sie doch. Sie ist sogar die Einzige, die da ist.

Hang on a minute, there she is. In fact, she's the only person who's present today.

lösen
['løːzən] *v*
to solve

Probleme lassen sich meist durch Nachdenken lösen.

Problems can usually be solved if you give them some thought.

ausbilden
['ausbɪldən] *v*
to train

Alex bildet Falken für die Jagd aus. Sei lieber nett zu den beiden.

Alex trains falcons to hunt. I'd be nice to both of them, if I were you.

die Seite
['zaɪtə] *n*
the page

Zufällig war das Buch auf der richtigen Seite aufgeschlagen.

The book just happened to be open at the right page.

üben
['yːbən] *v*
to practise

Schon ihnen beim Üben zuzusehen ist faszinierend.

Even watching them practise is fascinating.

das Heft
[hɛft] *n*
the exercise book

die Lektion
[lɛkˈtsjoːn] *n*
the lesson

die Lösung
['løːzʊŋ] *n*
the solution

richtig
[ʀɪçtɪç] *adj*
right

falsch
[falʃ] *adj*
wrong

sich irren
[zɪç 'ɪʀən] *v*
to be wrong

Ich denke, ich habe Zucker reingegeben und nicht Salz, aber ich kann mich auch irren.

I think I put sugar in rather than salt, but I could be wrong.

das Problem
[pʀoˈbleːm] *n*
the problem

Mit der Dosierung hat mein Mann immer Probleme.

My husband always seems to have a problem getting the quantity right.

der Fehler
['feːlɐ] *n*
the mistake

Ach, Fehler würde ich das nicht nennen. Das trägt man jetzt so.

Oh, I wouldn't call it a mistake. It's the fashion, these days.

fehlerfrei
['feːlɐfʀaɪ] *adj*
correct, accurate

Er war nicht sicher, ob er den Test fehlerfrei bestanden hatte.

He wasn't sure if he had done the test in a correct way.

sich verbessern
[zɪç fɛɐˈbɛsən] *v*
to improve

Wenn du deinem Bruder immer hilfst, wird er sich nie verbessern.

Your brother will never improve if you keep helping him.

die **Ausbildung**
['ausbɪldʊŋ] *n*
the training,
the instruction

durchfallen
['dʊrçfalən] *v*
to fail

Schon wieder durchgefallen.
Den Führerschein krieg' ich nie.

*Failed again. I'm never going
to get my licence.*

die **Sorgfalt**
['zɔrkfalt] *n*
the care

Bei so alten Autos ist
besondere Sorgfalt nötig.

*You need to take particular
care with cars this old.*

die **Aufmerk-
samkeit**
['aufmɛrkzaːmkaɪt] *n*
the attention

Ich erwarte von meinem Hund
absolute Aufmerksamkeit.

*I demand my dog's full
attention.*

ausgezeichnet
[ausgə'tsaɪçnət] *adj*
excellent

Für den Hauptgang eine aus-
gezeichnete Wahl, mein Herr.

*An excellent choice for your
main course, sir.*

THE COMPARATIVE FORMS OF „GUT" AND „SCHLECHT"

gut
[guːt] *adj, adv*
good, well

besser
['bɛse] *adj, adv*
better

am besten
[am 'bɛstən] *adj, adv*
best

schlecht
[ʃlɛçt] *adj, adv*
bad, badly

schlechter
['ʃlɛçte] *adj, adv*
worse

am schlechtesten
[am 'ʃlɛçtəstən] *adj, adv*
worst

sich anmelden
[zɪç ˈanmɛldən] *v*
to register

Echt? Du brauchst einen halben Tag, um dich anzumelden?

Does it really take half a day just to register?

das Zeugnis
[ˈtsɔyknɪs] *n*
the certificate

Jetzt hätte ich fast auch mein Zeugnis in die Luft geworfen.

I nearly threw my certificate in the air, too.

die Note
[ˈnoːtə] *n*
the mark, the grade

Kim hat wieder die besten Noten bekommen.

Kim got the best marks again.

die Prüfung
[ˈpryːfʊŋ] *n*
the examination

Abschreiben ist bei dieser Prüfung erheblich schwerer.

In this examination, copying is a lot harder.

Hör auf, alles zu wiederholen!

Hör du auf, alles zu wiederholen!

wiederholen
[viːdɛˈhoːlən] v
to repeat

Stop repeating everything!
You stop repeating everything!

schwierig, schwer
[ˈʃviːʁɪç], [ʃveːɐ] adj
difficult

Ab hier könnte der Abstieg schwierig werden.

The descent could get difficult from here on.

leicht, einfach
[laɪçt], [ˈaɪnfax] adj
easy

Lottes Lieblingsgericht geht ganz leicht.

Lotte's favourite dish is easy to make.

die **Anmeldung**
[ˈanmɛldʊŋ] n
the registration

die **Schwierigkeit**
[ˈʃviːʁɪçkaɪt] n
the difficulty

einfach
[ˈaɪnfax] adj
simple

der **Test**
[tɛst] n
the test

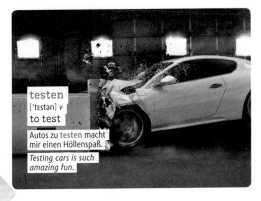

testen
[ˈtɛstən] v
to test

Autos zu testen macht mir einen Höllenspaß.

Testing cars is such amazing fun.

LANGUAGE

die **Sprache**
[ˈʃpʀaːxə] *n*
the language

Um die Sprache der Bienen
zu verstehen, muss man den
Bienentanz kennen.

*To understand the language of
bees, you need to learn about
their waggle dance.*

der Buchstabe
['buːxʃtabə] *n*
the letter

Mist! Meine Schreibmaschine hat nur kyrillische Buchstaben.

Damn, my typewriter only has Cyrillic letters.

bedeuten
[bə'dɔytən *v*
to mean

Papa, was bedeutet eigentlich „Transzendenz"?

Daddy, what does "transcendence" mean?

das Alphabet
[alfa'beːt] *n*
the alphabet

Mein Leon konnte schon mit eineinhalb das Alphabet!

My Leon knew his alphabet by the time he was eighteen months old!

übersetzen
[yːbɛ'zɛtsən] *v*
to translate

Martin Luther übersetzte die Bibel ins Deutsche.

Martin Luther translated the Bible into German.

das Wörterbuch
['vœrtebuːx] *n*
the dictionary

Schon immer hilfreich: ein Wörterbuch.

Always useful: a dictionary.

die Aussprache
['ausʃpraːxə] *n*
the pronunciation

Er versteht Japanisch sehr gut, kämpft aber noch mit der Aussprache.

He understands Japanese very well, but he struggles with the pronunciation.

der Text
[tɛkst] *n*
the text

Großmutter schreibt ihre Texte schon lange auf dem Computer.

Grandma has been writing her texts on the computer for quite a while now.

die Übersetzung
[yːbɛ'zɛtsʊŋ] *n*
the translation

die Bedeutung
[bə'dɔytʊŋ] *n*
the meaning

buchstabieren
[buːxʃta'biːrən] *v*
to spell

die Grammatik
[gra'matik] *n*
the grammar

das Wort
['vɔʀt] *n*
the word

der Satz
[zats] *n*
the sentence

das Substantiv
['zʊpstantiːf] *n*
the noun

das Verb
[vɛʀp] *n*
the verb

das Adjektiv
['atjɛktiːf] *n*
the adjective

das Adverb
['atvɛʀp] *n*
the adverb

die Einzahl
['aintsaːl] *n*
the singular

die Mehrzahl
['meːɐtsaːl] *n*
the plural

anrufen
['anru:fən], [telefo'ni:rən] *v*
to phone, to call

Aber natürlich, Chef, Sie
können mich jederzeit anrufen.

Of course, boss, you can
phone me any time you like.

das Telefon
[tele'fo:n] *n*
the (tele)phone

Mit dem neuen Telefon habe ich endlich die Hände frei.

Thanks to this new phone, my hands are finally free.

Dieses Handy ist garantiert abhörsicher. Hab' ich schließlich selbst gebaut.

This mobile phone is guaranteed bugproof. I did build it myself, after all.

das Handy, das Mobiltelefon
['hɛndi], [mo'bi:ltelefo:n] *n*
the mobile (phone)

wählen
['vɛ:lən] *v*
to dial

Für eine andere Warteschleifenmusik wählen Sie bitte folgende Nummer ...

To change the hold music, please dial the following number ...

telefonieren
[telefo'ni:rən] *v*
to make a phone call, to telephone

der Anruf
['anru:f] *n*
the call

besetzt
[bə'zɛtst] *adj*
engaged, busy

der Anrufbeantworter
['anru:fbeǀantvɔrte] *n*
the answerphone

die Vorwahl
['fo:eva:l] *n*
the dialling code, the area code

zurückrufen
[tsu'rʏkru:fən] *v*
to phone back

sich verwählen
[zɪç fɛɐ've:lən] *v*
to dial the wrong number

die Telefonnummer
[tele'fo:nnʊme] *n*
the telephone number

Moment, ich notiere nur schnell deine Telefonnummer.

Just a minute while I write your telephone number down.

der **Computer**
[kɔm'pjuːte] *n*
the computer

der **Bildschirm**
['bɪltʃɪrm] *n*
the screen

Nein, Sarah, du kannst jetzt nicht an den Computer. Ich muss arbeiten.

No, Sarah, you can't go on the computer now. I have to work.

die **DVD**
[deːfauˈdeː] *n*
the DVD

der **USB-Stick**
[uːˈɛsˈbeːstɪk] *n*
the USB stick

die **Taste**
['tastə] *n*
the key

die **Maus**
[maus] *n*
the mouse

die **Tastatur**
[tastaˈtuːe] *n*
the keyboard

die **E-Mail**
['iːmeɪl] *n*
the e-mail

Gib her, ich check die E-Mails.
Give it to me, I want to check my e-mails.

die **Festplatte**
['fɛstplatə] *n*
the hard disk

Die Festplatte muss gründlich gereinigt werden.
The hard disk needs a good clean-up.

das **Internet**
['ıntɛnɛt] *n*
the Internet

Was das Internet nicht findet,
existiert nicht. Oder?

*If you can't find it on the
Internet, it doesn't exist, right?*

die **Website**
['wɛbsaɪt] *n*
the website

Hier kann ich mich endlich
mal um meine Website
kümmern.

*At last, somewhere where
I can do my website.*

der **Drucker**
['drʊkɐ] *n*
the printer

ausdrucken
['aʊsdrʊkən] *v*
to print out

Einen Moment, ich
drucke noch eben einen
Eierbecher mit meinem
3-D-Drucker aus.

*Hang on, I'm just
printing an eggcup
out on my 3D printer.*

klicken
['klıkən] *v*
to click

Klicken Sie jetzt auf „absenden",
um den Betrag vom Konto ab-
buchen zu lassen.

*Click on "send" to debit your
account.*

der **Cursor**
['kø:ɐzɐ] *n*
the cursor

Wo der Cursor steht, darf
geschrieben werden.

*You can write where the
cursor is.*

HAL 2000, starte jetzt das Programm.

Es tut mir leid Francis, aber ich musste alle Daten löschen.

die Daten
['da:tən] *n*
the data

löschen
['lœʃən] *v*
to delete

das Programm
[pro'gram] *n*
the program

HAL 2000, start the program now.

I'm sorry, Francis, but I had to delete all data.

digital
[digi'ta:l] *adj*
digital

Das macht mir keiner nach: digitale Luftgitarre!

I'd like to see anyone else try this – digital air guitar!

kopieren
ko'pi:rən] *v*
to copy

Tommy kopiert immer nur die bekannteren Werke.

Tommy only ever copies the better-known works.

sichern, speichern
['zɪçən], ['ʃpaɪçən] *v*
to save

programmieren
[progra'mi:rən] *v*
to program

die Datei
[da'taɪ] *n*
the file

einfügen
['aɪnfy:gən] *v*
to paste

der Brief
[bri:f] *n*
the letter

Wäre dieser Brief nur 200 Jahre früher angekommen!

If only this letter had arrived 200 years sooner!

die Postleitzahl
['pɔstlaɪttsa:l] *n*
the postcode

So ein Mist. Schon wieder eine falsche Postleitzahl!

Unbelievable, another wrong postcode!

die Post
[pɔst] *n*
the post, the mail

die Briefmarke
[bʀi:fmaʀkə] *n*
the stamp

Meine Briefmarkensammlung sehe ich mir am liebsten alleine an.

I prefer to be alone when I'm looking through my stamp collection.

die Postkarte
['pɔstkartə] *n*
the postcard

Schreckliche Postkarte – genau die richtige für Tante Gertrud!

What an awful postcard – it's perfect for Auntie Gertrud!

schicken, senden
['ʃɪkən], ['zɛndən] *v*
to send

Stell dich nicht so an. So haben wir früher immer Nachrichten gesendet.

Stop making such a fuss. We always used to send messages like this in the past.

das Postamt
['pɔst|amt] *n*
the post office

Im Postamt wird aber auch jede Menge Ramsch verkauft.

They also sell loads of junk at the post office.

die **Information**
[ɪnfɔrma'tsjoːn] *n*
the information

Anscheinend will sie all diese Informationen mit niemandem teilen.

She doesn't look like she wants to share all that information with anyone.

senden
['zɛndən] *v*
to broadcast

Seit gestern senden wir mit dreifacher Leistung.

Since yesterday, we have tripled our broadcasting range.

der **Werbespot**
['vɛrbəspɔt] *n*
the commercial

Mit einem Fußball-Werbespot kann man alles verkaufen.

You can sell anything with a football commercial.

das **Programm**
[pro'gram] *n*
the programme

Schon wieder nur glückliche Kinder im Kinderprogramm.

Yet another children's programme with nothing but happy children.

das Radio
['ra:dio] *n*
the radio

Es heißt Radio, und YouTube
kann es nicht.

*It's called a radio and you can't
watch YouTube on it.*

fernsehen
['fɛrnze:ən] *v*
to watch TV

Oma lässt uns immer ganz
lange fernsehen.

*Our gran always lets us stay
up late to watch TV.*

das Fernsehen
['fɛrnze:ən] *n*
the television, the TV

Im Fernsehen vermischt sich
immer mehr Wahrheit mit Fiktion.

*It's getting harder and harder to tell
fact from fiction on TV these days.*

die **Zeitung**
['tsaɪtʊŋ] *n*
the (news)paper

Die Jungs von der Zeitung
waren natürlich schon alle da.

*Naturally, all the guys from
the newspaper were already there.*

die **Nachrichten**
['naːxrɪçtən] *n*
the news

Die Nachricht von seinem
Rücktritt verbreitete sich im Nu.

*The news of his resignation
spread like wildfire.*

die **Tageszeitung**
['taːgəstsaɪtʊŋ] *n*
the daily paper

Meine Tageszeitung ist noch
feucht, wenn ich sie bekomme.

*When I get my daily paper,
the print is still wet on the page.*

wahr
[vaːɐ] *adj*
true

Das ist alles **wahr**, dafür bürge ich mit meinem guten Ruf.

It's all true, I swear it on my reputation.

die Wahrheit
['vaːɐhaɪt] *n*
the truth

Sie wissen doch: Im Wein liegt die **Wahrheit**!

In wine there is truth, as they say!

die Ausgabe
['aʊsɡaːbə] *n*
the edition, the issue

In dieser alten **Ausgabe** hat schon Umberto Eco geblättert.

Umberto Eco has already been looking through this old edition.

das Abonnement
[abɔnə'mãː] *n*
the subscription

Seit ich das **Abonnement** habe, stapeln sich hier die Zeitungen.

The newspapers have been piling up since I took out a subscription.

der Artikel
[ar'tiːkəl] *n*
the article

Einen **Artikel** zu schreiben reicht nicht mehr, ich muss auch filmen …

It's no longer enough just to write an article, I have to get it on video too …

die Zeitschrift, die Illustrierte
['tsaɪtʃrɪft], [ɪlʊs'triːeta] *n*
the magazine

Hallo? Sie müssen die **Zeit**schrift erst kaufen, bevor Sie sie lesen.

Excuse me. You have to buy the magazine before you can read it.

informieren
[ɪnfɔr'miːrən] *v*
to inform

Und nun möchten wir Sie über ein paar gute Neuigkeiten **informieren**.

And now we would like to inform you of some good news.

PROFESSIONS

der **Beruf**
[bə'ʀuːf] *n*
the profession

Ach, das ist Ihr Beruf?
Kann man denn davon leben?

*Oh, so that's your
profession. Can you make
a living from that?*

beruflich
[bə'ru:flɪç] *adj*
professional

Ich bin eine berufliche Schönheit.

I'm a professional beauty.

arbeiten
['aʀbaɪtən] *v*
to work

Bis zu den Knien im Dreck: Das nenn' ich arbeiten!

Up to my knees in muck: that's what I call working!

die **Feuerwehr**
['fɔyevɛ:ɐ] *n*
the fire brigade

Knut wär' gern bei der Feuerwehr.

Knut would really like to join the fire brigade.

der **Anwalt**,
die **Anwältin**
['anvalt], ['anvɛltɪn] *n*
the lawyer

Ich spiele den Anwalt in einer Vorabendserie.

I play the lawyer in an early evening TV series.

der **Verkäufer**,
die **Verkäuferin**
[fɛɐ'kɔyfe], [fɛɐ'kɔyfaʀɪn] *n*
the shop assistant

Mal wieder ist nirgends ein Verkäufer zu sehen.

Yet again there isn't a shop assistant to be seen.

der **Polizist**,
die **Polizistin**
[poli'tsɪst], [poli'tsɪstɪn] *n*
the police officer

Die Polizistin versuchte, beruhigend aufzutreten.

The police officer tried to look reassuring.

der **Friseur**,
die **Friseurin**
[fri'zø:ɐ], [fri'zø:rɪn] *n*
the hairdresser

Die Kundin dieser Friseurin ist sehr viel geduldiger als andere.

The customer of this hairdresser is much more patient than others.

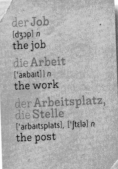

der **Job**
[dʒɔp] *n*
the job

die **Arbeit**
['aʀbaɪt] *n*
the work

der **Arbeitsplatz**,
die **Stelle**
['aʀbaɪtsplats], ['ʃtɛlə] *n*
the post

der **Arbeitnehmer,**
die **Arbeitnehmerin**
['arbaɪtneːmɐ], ['arbaɪtneːmərɪn] *n*
the employee

der **Arbeitgeber,**
die **Arbeitgeberin**
['arbaɪtgeːbɐ], ['arbaɪtgeːbərɪn] *n*
the employer

Unser Arbeitgeber hat eine ganz
spezielle Art zu motivieren.
*Our employer has a very special
way of motivating people.*

die **Anstellung,**
die **Beschäftigung**
['anʃtɛlʊŋ], [bəˈʃɛftɪɡʊŋ] *n*
the employment

Eine bessere Beschäftigung
habe ich nicht gefunden.
*I couldn't find any better
employment.*

einstellen
['aɪnʃtɛlən] *v*
to hire

Wir möchten Sie gerne als
Jugendbeauftragten einstellen.
*We'd very much like to hire you
as a youth representative.*

der **Kollege,**
die **Kollegin**
[kɔˈleːɡə], [koˈleːɡɪn] *n*
the colleague

Ich gebe meiner Kollegin
noch ein bisschen Arbeit ab –
die macht's gern.
*I'll hand over a bit more work to
my colleague – she'll love that.*

das **Team**
[tiːm] *n*
the team

Ein Team gibt einem Halt.
A team gives you support.

beschäftigen
[bəˈʃɛftɪɡən] *v*
to employ

die **Geschäfts-
leitung**
[ɡəˈʃɛftslaɪtʊŋ] *n*
the management

der **Mitarbeiter,**
die **Mitarbeiterin**
['mɪtʔarbaɪtɐ],
['mɪtʔarbaɪtərɪn] *n*
the co-worker

der Geschäftsführer,
die Geschäfts-
führerin
[gə'ʃɛftsfyːrɐ], [gə'ʃɛftsfyːrərɪn] *n*
the manager

Gut verhandelt: Wenn er als
Geschäftsführer versagt,
gibt es eine hohe Abfindung.

Good deal: if he fails as a
manager, he'll get a golden
handshake.

das Personal
[pɛrzo'naːl] *n*
the staff

Schlecht verhandelt: Wenn der
Geschäftsführer versagt, gibt es
beim Personal Lohnkürzungen.

Bad deal: if the manager fails,
the staff will get a pay cut.

So, Herr Kollege, fürs Zunähen sind jetzt Sie zuständig.

zuständig,
verantwortlich
['tsuːʃtɛndɪç],
[fɛɐ'|antvɔrtlɪç] *adj*
responsible

So, Doctor, now you're
responsible for sewing up.

arbeitslos
['arbaɪtsloːs] *adj*
unemployed

Dass Karl arbeitslos war,
freute als Einzigen den Hund.

Only the dog was happy that
Karl was unemployed.

leiten
['laɪtən] *v*
to run

Sie haben schon richtig
gesehen: ICH leite diese Firma.

You saw it right the first time:
I run this company.

Komm zur Gewerkschaft, hieß es, da kannst du was erleben …

die Gewerkschaft
[gə'vɛrkʃaft] *n*
the trade union

Come join the trade union, they said, you'll have a great time…

seinen Lebensunterhalt verdienen
[zaɪnən 'le:bənz|ʊntehalt fɛɐ'di:nən] *phrase*
to make a living

Als Beamter könnte ich **meinen Lebensunterhalt** viel leichter **verdienen**.

I could make a much easier living as a civil servant.

verdienen
[fɛɐ'di:nən] *v*
to earn

Für mich **verdient** meine App das Geld, ich muss nur wischen.

My app earns my money for me. I just need to do the swiping.

die Bewerbung
[bə'vɛrbʊŋ] *n*
the application

Vermaledeite Online-Bewerbung!

Blasted online application!

der Streik
[ʃtraɪk] *n*
the strike

Warten, bis der Streik beendet ist?
Da können wir ja gleich Bahn fahren!

Wait until the strike is over?
We might as well take the train!

die Forderung
[ˈfɔrdərʊŋ] *n*
the demand

Erfüllen Sie unsere Forderungen,
dann gibt es keine Probleme.

Meet our demands and there
won't be any problems.

das Gehalt
[gəˈhalt] *n*
the salary

Ich hab' nachgerechnet:
Mein Gehalt liegt noch
unter dem Mindestlohn!

I've checked the figures.
My salary is still lower than
the minimum wage!

die Rente
[ˈrɛntə] *n*
the pension

Mit meiner kümmerlichen
Rente kann ich mir den
Ruhestand nicht leisten.

I can't afford to retire on
my meagre pension.

der Ruhestand
[ˈruːəʃtant] *n*
the retirement

fordern
[ˈfɔrdən] *v*
to demand

sich bewerben
[zɪç bəˈvɛrbən] *v*
to apply

streiken
[ˈʃtraɪkən] *v*
to be on strike

das **Büro**
[by'ro:] *n*
the office

Hurra! Im neuen **Büro** hat jeder seinen eigenen **Schreibtisch**.

Hurray! In the new office everyone has their own desk.

der **Schreibtisch**
['ʃraɪptɪʃ] *n*
the desk

der **Stift**
[ʃtɪft] *n*
the pen

Für jede Aufgabe hat Mike einen speziellen **Stift**.

Mike has a special pen for every task.

der **Sekretär**, die **Sekretärin**
[zekre'tɛːe], [zekre'tɛːrɪn] *n*
the secretary

Doch, kommunikativ ist sie, unsere **Sekretärin**.

Oh no, our secretary is communicative all right.

der **Kopierer**
[ko'piːre] *n*
the photocopier

Bernhard macht seine Passbilder immer nur auf dem **Kopierer**.

For his passport photos Bernhard will only ever use the photocopier.

die Unterlagen
['ʊntelaːgən] *n*
the documents

Irgendwo in den Unterlagen muss die Karte vom Pizzaservice sein.

The menu for the pizza delivery service must be somewhere in these documents.

die Visitenkarte
[viˈziːtənkaʀtə] *n*
the business card

Auf der Visitenkarte steht alles, was Sie über mich wissen müssen.

Everything you need to know about me is on my business card.

schreiben
[ˈʃʀaɪbən] *v*
to write

Mit der Hand zu schreiben lässt die Gedanken freier fließen.

Writing by hand makes your thoughts flow more freely.

FEBRUARY
29
FEBRUARY

der Kalender
[kaˈlɛndə] *n*
the diary, the calendar

Mit dem Februar in diesem Kalender stimmt etwas nicht.

die Notiz
[noˈtiːts] *n*
the note

There's something wrong with February in this diary.

das Papier
[paˈpiːɐ] *n*
the paper

Papier kann sich nicht aussuchen, womit es bedruckt wird.

Paper doesn't get to choose what's printed on it.

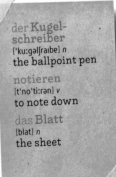

der Kugelschreiber
[ˈkuːgəlʃʀaɪbɐ] *n*
the ballpoint pen

notieren
[tˈnoˈtiːʀən] *v*
to note down

das Blatt
[blat] *n*
the sheet

EATING & DRINKING

die **Lebensmittel**
['leːbənsmɪtəl] *n*
the food

Wir werfen keine Lebensmittel
weg – wir essen sie alle auf!

*We don't throw any food
away – we eat it all up!*

essen
['ɛsən] *v*
to eat

So lustig war es noch
nie, Spinat zu essen!

*Eating spinach
has never been so
much fun!*

der **Hunger**
['hʊŋə] *n*
the hunger

Ihr Hunger trieb die kleine
Raupe voran.

*It was hunger that drove the
little caterpillar on.*

trinken
['tʀɪŋkən] *v*
to drink

Nachmittags trinkt Akono gerne
mal einen über den Durst.

*Akono likes to drink one too
many in the afternoons.*

der **Durst**
['dʊrst] *n*
the thirst

Ich ging weiter und weiter und versuchte, meinen Durst zu vergessen.

*I walked on and on, trying to
forget my thirst.*

hungrig
['hʊŋɡrɪç] *adj*
hungry

durstig
['dʊrstɪç] *adj*
thirsty

die **Mahlzeit**
['maːltsaɪt] *n*
the meal

Guten Appetit!
[guːtən apeˈtiːt] *phrase*
Enjoy your
meal!

der **Appetit**
[apeˈtiːt] *n*
the appetite

Die Vorspeise ist viel zu wenig –
gemessen an seinem Appetit …

*This starter will be nowhere
near enough – going on his
appetite…*

Prost!
[proːst] *interj*
Cheers!

Endlich: Der Chef hat
aufgegeben. Prost!

*At last, the boss has
given up. Cheers!*

scharf
[ʃaʁf] *adj*
hot, spicy

Nimm nicht alle, ich mag es nicht so scharf.

Don't use them all. I don't like it so spicy.

sauer
[ˈzauɐ] *adj*
sour

Sonja liebt es sauer.

Sonja loves anything sour.

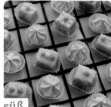

süß
[zyːs] *adj*
sweet

Hüftgold nennt man diese süßen Teile.

These sweet things are called love handles.

Ich bleibe dabei: Diese Suppe schmeckt wie alte Socken.

schmecken
[ˈʃmɛkən] *v*
to taste

I still think this soup tastes like old socks.

kochen
['kɔxən] v
to cook, to boil

Samstags übe ich mit meiner Schwester kochen.

On Saturdays I practise cooking with my sister.

Kochen means „to boil" (a liquid) as well as „to cook" (food). In English „to cook" can also be used for other methods of preparation as well as boiling, such as frying, grilling and baking. In German however the specific word is needed for each method: *braten*, *grillen* and *backen* respectively.

schneiden
[ʃnaidən] v
to cut

Diese Säge schneidet Hartholz wie Butter.

This saw cuts through hardwood like butter.

tiefgekühlt, Tiefkühl-
['tiːfgəkyːlt], ['tiːfkyːl] *adj*
frozen

Wer auch im Winter Beeren will, muss Tiefkühlware nehmen.

If you want to have berries in winter too, you have to get frozen ones.

roh
['roː] *adj*
raw

Ich mache die Steinzeit-Diät: alles roh, aber mit Stil.

I'm on the Stone Age diet: raw food only but done in style.

frisch
[frɪʃ] *adj*
fresh

köstlich
['kœstlɪç] *adj*
delicious

zubereiten
['tsuːbəraitən] v
to make

warm machen
['varm 'maxən] v
to warm up

gar
[gaːe] *adj*
cooked

Natürlich sind die Pilze heiß, sonst wären sie ja nicht gar.

Of course the mushrooms are hot. They wouldn't be cooked otherwise.

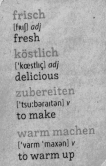

das **Brot**
[bro:t] *n*
the bread

Ich traue diesen Backshops nicht –
ich mach' mein Brot selber.

*I don't trust these bakeries –
I make my own bread.*

das **Stück**
[ʃtʏk] *n*
the piece

Ach nein, bitte nur ein ganz
kleines Stück!

*Oh no, just a very small piece,
please!*

die **Nudeln**
['nu:dəln] *n*
the noodles, the pasta

In Japan darf man die Nudeln
auch schlürfen.

*In Japan you're allowed to slurp
your noodles too.*

der **Reis**
[raɪs] *n*
the rice

Mit Trüffeln wird simpler Reis
zur Haute Cuisine.

*Truffles turn simple rice into
haute cuisine.*

der **Keks**
[ke:ks] *n*
the biscuit,
the cookie

Bei uns lebt ein Geist, der Kekse
verschwinden lässt.

*There's a ghost living in our
house that makes biscuits
disappear.*

die **Torte**
['tɔrtə] *n*
the gateau

die **Scheibe**
['ʃaɪbə] *n*
the slice

das **Brötchen**
['brø:tçən] *n*
the roll

der **Kuchen**
['ku:xən] *n*
the cake

Wie bitte? Unsere Kuchen
schmecken Ihnen nicht?

*I beg your pardon?
You don't like our cakes?*

das Gemüse
[gəˈmyːzə] *n*
the vegetable

Gemüse aller Länder, vereinigt euch!

Vegetables of the world, unite!

die **Kartoffel**
[karˈtɔfəl] *n*
the potato

die **Möhre**
[ˈmøːrə] *n*
the carrot

die **Gurke**
[ˈgʊrkə] *n*
the cucumber

der **Mais**
[maɪs] *n*
the sweetcorn

die **Paprika**
[ˈpapʀika] *n*
the pepper

die **Tomate**
[toˈmaːtə] *n*
the tomato

Die roten Tomaten landen heute Abend im Salat.

The red tomatoes will go in tonight's salad.

die **Zwiebel**
[ˈtsviːbəl] *n*
the onion

Ich hasse es, Zwiebeln zu schneiden.

I hate chopping onions!

die **Olive**
[oˈliːvə] *n*
the olive

Gerührt oder geschüttelt? Egal, Hauptsache mit Olive.

Shaken or stirred? I don't mind, as long as you put an olive in it.

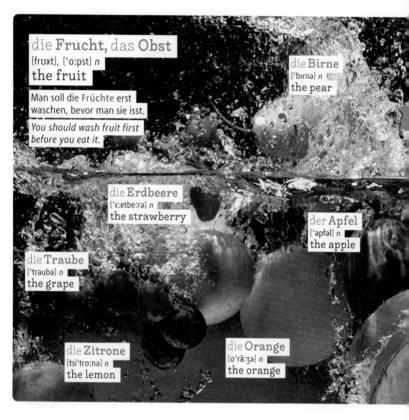

die Frucht, das Obst
[frʊxt], ['oːpst] *n*
the fruit

Man soll die Früchte erst
waschen, bevor man sie isst.
You should wash fruit first
before you eat it.

die Birne
['bɪrnə] *n*
the pear

die Erdbeere
['ɛːetbeːrə] *n*
the strawberry

der Apfel
['apfəl] *n*
the apple

die Traube
['traubə] *n*
the grape

die Zitrone
[tsi'troːnə] *n*
the lemon

die Orange
[oˈrãːʒə] *n*
the orange

der Pfirsich
['pfɪrzɪçʃ] *n*
the peach

Der Pfirsich erinnert mich an
Helgas Haut von vor 60 Jahren.
This peach reminds me of
Helga's skin 60 years ago.

die Kirsche
['kɪrʃə] *n*
the cherry

Ich mag nur die Kirsche,
du kannst den Rest haben.
I only like the cherry.
You can have the rest.

die Banane
[baˈnaːnə] *n*
the banana

Bananen schäle ich locker
mit Händen und Füßen.
I can easily peel bananas
with my hands or my feet.

das **Fleisch**
[flaɪʃ] *n*
the meat

Ich kann dir gleich sagen, ob man das Fleisch noch essen kann.

I'll be able to tell you in just a moment if the meat's still edible.

das **Schweinefleisch**
[ˈʃvaɪnəflaɪʃ] *n*
the pork

Schweinefleisch? Bitte entlang der Linien ausschneiden.

Pork? Please cut along the dotted lines.

das **Hühnchen**
[ˈhyːnçən] *n*
the chicken

Gut, dass wir unser Hühnchen nicht selber rupfen müssen.

It's a good thing we don't have to pluck our own chicken.

das **Rindfleisch**
[ˈrɪntflaɪʃ] *n*
the beef

Oma hält nichts von der Steinzeit-Diät und schmort das Rindfleisch ausgiebig.

Grandma's not a fan of the Stone Age diet and braises beef for a long time.

das **Kalbfleisch**
[ˈkalpflaɪʃ] *n*
the veal

der **Speck**
[ʃpɛk] *n*
the bacon

die **Salami**
[ˈzalaːmi] *n*
the salami

der **Schinken**
[ˈʃɪŋkən] *n*
the ham

das **Steak**
[steːk] *n*
the steak

Außen braun und innen rot: So mag ich mein Steak!

Brown on the outside and red on the inside. That's how I like my steak!

die **Wurst**
[vʊrst] *n*
the sausage

Alles hat ein Ende, nur die Wurst hat keines.

Everything comes to an end. Apart from sausages.

der Essig
['ɛsɪç] *n*
the vinegar

Dieser Essig reift zwölf
Jahre im Fass.

*This vinegar is matured in
a barrel for twelve years.*

das Öl
[ø:l] *n*
the oil

Mein Auto fährt sicher auch
mit Salatöl.

*I'm sure my car will run on
salad oil too.*

der Lachs
[laxs] *n*
the salmon

Der Lachs hatte sich bei seinem
Sprung katastrophal verschätzt.

*The salmon had made
a fatal mistake in its leap.*

die Garnele
[gar'ne:lə] *n*
the prawn

Die Garnele ist die
unangefochtene Herrin
des Aquariums.

*The prawn is the
undisputed boss of
the aquarium.*

der Thunfisch
['tu:nfɪʃ] *n*
the tuna

Das armselige Ende eines
ehemals stolzen Thunfischs.

*The pitiful end of a once
proud tuna.*

die Milch
[mɪlç] *n*
the milk

Diese Milch ist wirklich einzigartig.

There's nothing quite like this milk.

die Sahne
['zaːnə] *n*
the cream

Entweder richtige Sahne oder gar keine Torte!

The cake is either made with real cream or you might as well forget it!

die Butter
['bʊtɐ] *n*
the butter

Butter und Salz – mehr brauch' ich nicht aufs Brot.

Butter and salt – that's all I need on my bread.

der Käse
['kɛːzə] *n*
the cheese

Der Geruch nach Käse stört einen nur am Anfang.

The smell of cheese only bothers you at the start.

das Salz
[zalts] *n*
the salt

Hier ist genug Salz für dein Frühstücksei: Bedien dich einfach.

There's enough salt here for your breakfast egg. Just help yourself.

das Ei
[aɪ] *n*
the egg

Eier richtig aufzuschlagen ist eine Kunst.

There's an art to breaking eggs properly.

das Eigelb
['aɪgɛlp] *n*
the (egg) yolk

das Eiweiß
['aɪvaɪs] *n*
the egg white

das Bonbon
[bɔŋˈbɔŋ] n
the sweet,
the (piece of) candy

Bitte nur rosa Bonbons für
mich!

Only pink sweets for me, please!

das Eis
[aɪs] n
the ice cream

Lisa hätte auch gern bunte
Stückchen auf ihrem Eis.

*Lisa would have liked her ice cream
to have colourful bits too.*

die Konfitüre
[kɔnfiˈtyːrə] n
the jam

Greifen Sie zu!
Alle Konfitüren
sind hausgemacht.

*Tuck in! All the jams
are homemade.*

die Marmelade
[marməˈlaːdə] n
the marmalade

die Schokolade
[ʃokoˈlaːdə] n
the chocolate

Schokolade in Kaskaden – der
Hit auf jedem Kindergeburtstag.

*A chocolate fountain – a hit at
any children's birthday party.*

der Zucker
[ˈtsʊkɐ] n
the sugar

Musst du den Zucker immer
umwerfen?

*Do you always have to knock
over the sugar?*

der Honig
[ˈhoːnɪç] n
the honey

Ich mag keinen Zucker, ich nehme nur ganz frischen Honig.

*I don't like sugar. I only eat
really fresh honey.*

das Getränk
[gəˈtrɛŋk] n
the drink

Für Marina gibt es nur noch
farblose Getränke.

*Marina's only having colourless
drinks from now on.*

der **Eiswürfel**
['aɪsvʏrfəl] *n*
the ice cubel

Eiswürfel sind die kalorienarme Variante von Eiscreme.

Ice cubes are the low-calorie equivalent of ice cream.

das **Mineralwasser**
[mine'ra:lvase] *n*
the mineral water

Ohne eine Flasche Mineralwasser gehe ich nicht aus dem Haus.

I don't leave the house without a bottle of mineral water.

der **Wein**
[vaɪn] *n*
the wine

Wer **Wein** haben will, muss die Trauben kaputt machen.

If you want wine, you have to crush the grapes.

He, Finger weg von meinem Bier!

das **Bier**
['bi:ɐ] *n*
the beer

Hey, hands off my beer!

die **Flasche**
['flaʃə] *n*
the bottle

… Aber versuch bloß nicht, ihr die **Flasche** wegzunehmen.

…But just don't try taking the bottle away from her.

der **Kaffee**
['kafe] *n*
the coffee

In der Werbung machen sie die Bläschen auf dem **Kaffee** mit Spülmittel.

In coffee adverts they use washing-up liquid to make the froth.

der **Tee**
[te:] *n*
the tea

Für diese Art, **Tee** zu trinken, müssen Sie sich Zeit nehmen.

You have to take your time to drink tea like this.

der **Alkohol**
['alkoho:l] *n*
the alcohol

die **Limonade**
[limo'na:də] *n*
the lemonade

der **Saft**
[zaft] *n*
the juice

der **Drink**
[drɪŋk] *n*
the drink

GOING OUT

das **Restaurant**
[rɛstoˈrã] *n*
the restaurant

Im Restaurant muss man
auch bei vielen Bestellungen
die Qualität halten.

*In a restaurant you have to
maintain the quality even
when there are lots of orders.*

die **Bedienung**
[bə'di:nʊŋ] *n*
the waitress

die **Speisekarte**
['ʃpaɪzəkartə] *n*
the menu

Es steht nicht auf der
Speisekarte, aber dürfte
ich Sie bitten …
*It's not on the menu,
but might I request…?*

der **Kellner,**
der **Ober**
['kɛlnɐ], ['o:bɐ] *n*
the waiter

Hallooooo! Herr Ober!
Yoohoo! Waiter!

das **Trinkgeld**
['trɪŋkgɛlt] *n*
the tip

Das soll ein Trinkgeld sein?
Is that supposed to be a tip?

nur
[nu:ɐ] *adv*
only

… ich hab' ja auch nur wenig
Hunger.
*…I'm only slightly hungry
anyway.*

die **Rechnung**
['rɛçnʊŋ] *n*
the bill

Das muss die Rechnung für
den Nebentisch sein.
*That must be the bill for the
next table.*

bezahlen
[bə'tsa:lən] *v*
to pay

Ich habe Sie für Ihren Job
bezahlt, jetzt verschwinden Sie!
*I've paid you for your work,
now beat it!*

das Café
[kaˈfeː] n
the café

Martha war froh, dass Inge ihr im Café keine Szene machte.

Martha was glad that Inge didn't make a scene at the café.

die Konditorei
[kɔnditoˈraɪ] n
the cake shop

Shopping-Frust? In der Konditorei findest du immer etwas.

Can't find what you're looking for? You'll always find something at the cake shop.

der Nachtisch
[ˈnaːxtɪʃ] n
the dessert

Lass uns den Nachtisch teilen: Du kriegst das Minzeblättchen.

Let's share the dessert. You can have the mint leaf.

das Menü
[meˈny] n
the set meal

Oh Gott, das Menü besteht aus 19 Gängen.

Oh God, the set meal is made up of 19 courses..

der Gang
[gaŋ] n
the course

das Gericht
[gəˈrɪçt] n
the dish

die Kneipe
[ˈknaɪpə] n
the pub

die Bar
[ˈbaːɐ] n
the bar

die Imbissbude
[ˈɪmbɪsbuːdə] n
the snack bar

die **Suppe**
['zʊpə] *n*
the soup

Suppe für 40 Mann – das ist ein
echter Kraftakt.

*Soup for 40 – that's a real feat
of strength.*

die **Spezialität**
[ʃpetsjali'tɛːt] *n*
the speciality

Diese Spezialität bekomme ich
nur mit einem Schnaps runter.

*The only way I can get
this speciality down is with
some schnapps.*

das **Omelett**
['ɔmlɛt] *n*
the omelette

Halbfinale bei der
Weltmeisterschaft im
Omelettzubereiten.

*Semi-final of the World
Omelette-Making
Championships.*

die **Pommes frites**
[pɔm 'fʀit] *n*
the chips,
the French fries

Diese Engländer: Schütten Essig
auf ihre Pommes frites!

*These English people. Putting
vinegar on their chips!*

der **Imbiss**
['ɪmbɪs] *n*
the snack

der **Hamburger**
['hambʊrgɐ] *n*
the hamburger

die **Pizza**
['pɪtsa] *n*
the pizza

das **Sandwich**
['zɛntvɪtʃ] *n*
the sandwich

das Frühstück
['fry:ʃtvk] *n*
the breakfast

Zeigst du mir nach dem Frühstück endlich deine Briefmarkensammlung?

Are you finally going to show me your stamp collection after breakfast?

reservieren
[REZER'vi:ʀən] *v*
to reserve, to book

Gerne reserviere ich Ihnen die Caligula-Suite.

I'd be happy to book the Caligula Suite for you.

den Tisch decken
['tɪʃ dɛkən] *phrase*
to set the table

Wenn ich die **Tische decke**, ist das fast wie eine Meditation.

When I'm setting the tables, it's almost like doing meditation.

das Mittagessen
['mɪta:k|ɛsən] *n*
the lunch

Tanja genießt das gemeinsame Mittagessen mit André.

Tanja enjoys having lunch with André.

das Abendessen
['a:bənt|ɛsən] *n*
the supper, the dinner

Schatzi, beeil dich mit dem Abendessen, die Flut kommt.

Hurry up with your dinner, darling. The tide's coming in.

frühstücken
['fʀy:ʃtvkən] *v*
to have breakfast

zu Mittag essen
[tsu: 'mɪta:k 'ɛsən] *phrase*
to have lunch

zu Abend essen
[tsu: 'a:bənt 'ɛsən] *phrase*
to have dinner

voll
[fɔl] *adj*
full

Kaum wird der Mond **voll**, sprießen mir die Haare und wachsen die Zähne.

As soon as the moon is full I sprout hair and my teeth start to grow.

leer
[leːɐ] *adj*
empty

Jeden Morgen müssen wir die leeren Flaschen wegbringen.

We have to get rid of the empty bottles every morning.

ohne
[ˈoːnə] *prep*
without

Ich trinke meinen Kaffee ohne Zucker...

I take my coffee without sugar...

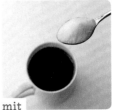

mit
[mɪt] *prep*
with

... obwohl, bei diesem hier doch lieber mit.

...but in this case I prefer it with.

Viel Spaß!
['fi:l 'ʃpa:s] *interj*
Have fun!

Egon ist auch auf der Party?
Na dann viel Spaß!

Egon's also at the party?
Oh well then, have fun!

War eine gute Idee, mit Heidi auszugehen. Das verspricht amüsant zu werden.

ausgehen
['ausge:ən] *v*
to go out

Going out with Heidi was a good idea. This promises to be funny.

amüsant
[amy'zant] *adj*
funny

das Geschenk
[gə'ʃɛŋk] *n*
the present

Ein Geschenk? Für mich?
Danke, Omi!

A present? For me?
Thanks, Grandma!

der Geburtstag
[gə'bu:etsta:k] *n*
the birthday

Sie hat Geburtstag, aber so richtig freuen kann sie sich nicht.

It's her birthday but she can't really enjoy it.

gratulieren
[gratu'li:rən] *v*
to congratulate

Ich darf Ihnen zu Ihrem Jodeldiplom gratulieren.

May I congratulate you on your yodelling diploma.

betrunken
[bə'truŋkən] *adj*
drunk

Am Ende von Helens Party waren wir alle betrunken.

At the end of Helen's party, we were all drunk.

das Fest, die Party
[fɛst], ['pa:eti] *n*
the party

Unerkannt schlich sich der Tod auf Antons Halloween-Party.

Death was on the prowl incognito at Anton's Halloween party.

tanzen
['tantsən] *v*
to dance

Hey Dolly. That's the last time that guy's dancing with you…

Hey Dolly, das ist das letzte Mal, dass der Typ mit dir tanzt…

genießen
[gə'ni:sən] *v*
to enjoy

rauchen
[ʀauxən] *v*
to smoke

Hier kann ich rauchen und darf es auch noch genießen.
Hier kann ich rauchen und darf es auch noch genießen.

sich amüsieren
[zɪç amy'zi:rən] *v*
to enjoy oneself

der Tanz
[tants] *n*
the dance

feiern
['faien] *v*
to celebrate

einen trinken gehen
[aɪnən 'trɪŋkən ge:ən] *phrase*
to go for a drink

die **Kunst**
[kʊnst] *n*
the art

Die Kunst ist eine Vermittlerin
des Unaussprechlichen.

*Art is a conduit for the
inexpressible.*

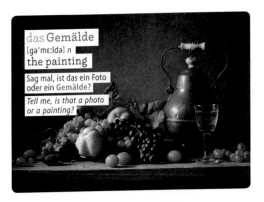

das Gemälde
[gə'mɛːldə] *n*
the painting

Sag mal, ist das ein Foto oder ein Gemälde?

Tell me, is that a photo or a painting?

das Atelier
[atə'lje:] *n*
the studio

Die Miete für Amelies Atelier bezahlt Onkel Gustav.

Uncle Gustav pays the rent for Amelie's studio.

zeichnen
['tsaɪçnən] *v*
to draw

Larry liebt es, seinen Freund zu zeichnen.

Larry loves drawing his friend.

die Galerie
[galə'riː] *n*
the gallery

Die Galerie machte an diesem Tag den halben Jahresumsatz.

The gallery made half its annual turnover that day.

So wird aus einer antiken Figur moderne Kunst.

That's how you make modern art out of an ancient statue.

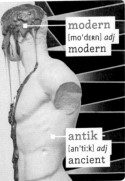

modern
[mo'dɛʀn] *adj*
modern

antik
[an'tiːk] *adj*
ancient

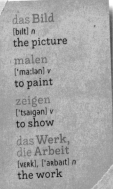

das Bild
[bɪlt] *n*
the picture

malen
['maːlən] *v*
to paint

zeigen
['tsaɪɡən] *v*
to show

das Werk, die Arbeit
[vɛʀk], ['aʀbaɪt] *n*
the work

das **Theater**
[te'aːtɐ] *n*
the theatre

Das Meiste im Theater verstehe ich nicht, aber ich gucke gerne zu.

I don't understand most of what goes on at the theatre but I like to watch.

die **Bühne**
['byːnə] *n*
the stage

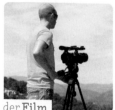

der **Film**
[fɪlm] *n*
the film

Schluss mit Hollywood. Ich mach' jetzt meinen eigenen Film.

I'm through with Hollywood. Now I'm going to make my own film.

das **Kino**
['kiːno] *n*
the cinema

Im Kino wird sie wenigstens satt.

At least she'll eat her fill at the cinema.

das **Theaterstück**
[te'aːtɐʃtyk] *n*
the play

die **Vorstellung**,
die **Aufführung**
['foːrʃtɛlʊŋ], ['aʊffyːrʊŋ] *n*
the performance

inszenieren
[ɪnstse'niːrən] *v*
to stage

die **Handlung**
['handlʊŋ] *n*
the plot

das **Buch**
[buːx] *n*
the book

Ich hatte das Gefühl, dass das Buch mich veränderte.

I had the feeling that the book was changing me.

lesen
[ˈleːzən] *v*
to read

Nur der Scanner kann hier die Preise lesen.

Only the scanner gets to read the prices here.

der **Roman**
[ʀoˈmaːn] *n*
the novel

Wie hieß noch mal dieser Roman mit dem Wal?

What was that novel about the whale called again?

die **Bücherei,**
die **Bibliothek**
[byçəˈʀaɪ], [biblioˈteːk] *n*
the library

Jamie bekam daraufhin Hausverbot in der Bücherei.

Jamie was banned from the library after that.

das **Märchen**
[ˈmɛːeçən] *n*
the fairy tale

Der König hätte am liebsten in einem Märchen gelebt.

The king would have liked most of all to live in a fairy tale.

der **Leser,**
die **Leserin**
[ˈleːzɐ], [ˈleːzəʀɪn] *n*
the reader

der **Titel**
[ˈtiːtəl] *n*
the title

die **Geschichte**
[ɡəˈʃɪçtə] *n*
the story

die **Erzählung**
[ɛɐˈtsɛːlʊŋ] *n*
the tale

Hey, die Kinder haben echt ein Gefühl für Musik.

die Musik
[muˈziːk] *n*
the music

Hey, the kids have got a real feeling for music.

die Stimme
[ˈʃtɪmə] *n*
the voice

Unglaublich, was sie mit ihrer Stimme vermag.

It's unbelievable what she can do with her voice.

das Konzert
[kɔnˈtsɛrt] *n*
the concert

Das war das tollste Konzert seines Lebens.

It was the most fantastic concert of his life.

die Oper
[ˈoːpe] *n*
the opera

In dieser Oper verstehe ich den Text überhaupt nicht.

I don't understand the words to this opera at all.

singen
['zɪŋən] v
to sing

Gudrun sang die Brunhilde
voll Inbrunst.

*Gudrun sang the role of
Brunhilde with great fervour.*

die Stereoanlage
['ʃteːreoˌanlaːgə] n
the stereo

Kennst du dich noch mit so
Stereoanlagen aus?

*Do you still know how to work
things like stereos?*

der Lautsprecher
['lautʃprɛçɐ] n
the loudspeaker

Einer dieser Lautsprecher
müsste doch funktionieren.

*One of these loudspeakers
has got to work.*

das Lied
[liːt] n
the song

Ich habe dir ein Lied geschrieben. Kommst du zu mir zurück?

*I've written you a song. Will you
come back to me*

laut
[laut] adv
loud

Der Pfeifton in meinem
Ohr ist seit den Bauarbeiten
richtig laut geworden.

*That whistling sound in my ear
has got really loud since the
construction work began.*

leise
['laɪzə] adv
quiet

Seien Sie leise.
Die Chefin meditiert.

*Be quiet.
The boss is meditating.*

das **Instrument**
[ɪnstruˈmɛnt] *n*
das Instrument

Ich muss wahrscheinlich noch ein anderes Instrument lernen.

I should probably learn to play another instrument.

das **Klavier**
[klaˈviːɐ] *n*
the piano

Wenn Walter Klavier spielt, ist Waldi sein schärfster Kritiker.

When Walter plays the piano, Waldi is his fiercest critic.

die **Gitarre**
[giˈtarə] *n*
the guitar

Nie wollte er Bauer werden, er wollte immer nur Gitarre spielen.

He'd never wanted to be a farmer. He'd only ever wanted to play the guitar.

das **Schlagzeug**
[ˈʃlaːktsɔyk] *n*
the drums

Mein Schlagzeug macht mir die Haare schön.

My drums make my hair look beautiful.

die **Trommel**
[ˈtrɔməl] *n*
the drum

Die Trommel geht mir langsam auf die Nerven.

That drum is starting to get on my nerves.

das Orchester
[ˈɔʀkɛstɐ] n
the orchestra

Das Orchester war auf der Suche nach dem Rhythmus.

The orchestra was searching for the rhythm.

der Bass
[bas] n
the bass

die Geige, die Violine
[ˈɡaɪɡə], [vioˈliːnə] n
the violin

spielen
[ˈʃpiːlən] v
to play

die Flöte
[ˈfløːtə] n
the flute

hoch
[hoːx] adj
high

Das hohe Zwitschern des Blaukehlchens …

The high twittering of the Bluethroat…

tief
[tiːf] adj
low

… wird prompt mit tiefem Röhren des See-Elefanten beantwortet.

…is promptly answered by the low roaring of the Elephant Seal.

SHOPPING

das **Geschäft**,
der **Laden**
[gə'ʃɛft], ['laːdən] *n*
the shop

Ich möchte nicht
wissen, was die Läden
hier an Miete zahlen.

*I wouldn't like to know
how much the shops
pay in rent here.*

Tss. Was man in dieser Buch-handlung so alles unter Kinder-büchern versteht…

die Buch-handlung
['buːxhandlʊŋ] *n*
the book shop

Tut tut. The things they call children's books in this book shop…

der Markt
[maʀkt] *n*
the market

Auf dieser Art von Markt herrscht noch Realwirtschaft.
The real economy still rules at this type of market.

die Bäckerei
[bɛkəˈʀaɪ] *n*
the bakery

In meiner Bäckerei gibt es kein Vollkornbrot! Basta!
My bakery doesn't have any wholemeal bread! That does it!

das Kaufhaus
['kaufhaus] *n*
the department store

Die Spielsachen sind aber in diesem Kaufhaus ganz oben…
But the toys are right on the top floor of this department store…

der Supermarkt
['zuːpemaʀkt] *n*
the supermarket

Ich bin gerade im Supermarkt. Brauchst du was?
I'm just at the supermarket. Do you need anything?

das Lebensmittel-geschäft
['leːbənsmɪtəlɡəʃɛft] *n*
the grocery

das Schuhgeschäft
['ʃuːɡəʃɛft] *n*
the shoe shop

das Bekleidungs-geschäft
[bəˈklaɪdʊŋsɡəʃɛft] *n*
the clothes shop

die Einkaufstasche
['aɪŋkaufstaʃə] *n*
the shopping bag

Was hast du in deiner
Einkaufstasche? – In welcher?

*What have you got in your
shopping bag? – Which one?*

kaufen
['kaufən] *v*
to buy

Nein, Lennart, man kauft Kinder
doch nicht im Supermarkt.

*No, Lennart, you don't buy
children at the supermarket.*

geschlossen
[gə'ʃlɔsən] *adj*
closed

geöffnet, offen
[gə'|œfnət], [ɔfən] *adj*
open

Warum ist dieser Fensterladen
immer nur kurz geöffnet?

*Why is this shutter only
ever open for a short time?*

verkaufen
[fɛɐ'kaufən] *v*
to sell

Ganz diskret verkaufte Christina
ihren Hochzeitsschmuck.

*Christina sold her wedding
jewellery very discreetly.*

der Einkaufszettel
['aɪnkaufststsetəl] *n*
the shopping list

Tanjas Einkaufszettel ist digital,
weil sie ihn so nicht verliert.

*Tanja's shopping list is digital
because that way she can't
lose it.*

aussuchen
['ausˌzuːxən] v
to choose

Man muss sich seine Freunde
sorgfältig aussuchen.

*You have to choose your
friends carefully.*

vollständig
['fɔlʃtɛndɪç] adj
complete

Klein, aber vollständig!

Small but complete!

ausverkauft
['ausfɛɐkauft] adj
sold out

Das Vollkornbrot war wider
Erwarten ausverkauft.

*The wholemeal bread was
unexpectedly sold out.*

neu
[nɔy] adj
new

Mein neues Auto. Bald.
Ich fange schon an zu sparen.

*My new car. Or it soon will be.
I've already started saving up.*

gebraucht
[ɡəˈbrauxt] adj
second-hand

Hier gibt's sogar
gebrauchte Glühbirnen!

*You can even get second-
hand light bulbs here!*

bedienen
[baˈdiːnən] v
to serve

der Verkauf
[fɛɐˈkauf] n
the sale

der Kauf
[kauf] n
the acquisition

das Angebot
['anɡaboːt] n
the offer

billig
['bılıç] *adj*
cheap

In Rom hatten wir Gott sei Dank
ein billiges Hotel gefunden.
*Thank God we'd found a cheap
hotel in Rome.*

die Reklamation
[reklama'tsjoːn] *n*
the complaint

Viktoria hatte eine Reklamation
wegen der Tassengröße.
*Viktoria made a complaint
about the size of the cup.*

War deine
Nasen-OP
auch so teuer?

teuer
['tɔye] *adj*
expensive

*Was your nose job so
expensive too?*

die (Warte)Schlange
['(vartə)ʃlaŋə] *n*
the queue

An der Herrentoilette war
wieder mal eine lange Schlange.
*There was a long queue for
the gents again.*

kosten
['kɔstən] *v*
to cost

reklamieren
[rekla'miːrən] *v*
to query

Was kostet ...?
['vas 'kɔstət ...] *phrase*
How much is...?

die Quittung,
der Beleg
['kvıtʊŋ], [bə'leːk] *n*
the receipt

ausgeben
['ausge:bən] *v*
to spend

Wollen Sie wirklich alle Gold-Nuggets für Seife ausgeben?

Do you really want to spend all your gold nuggets on soap?

der Preis
[prais] *n*
the price

Warte bis es hagelt, dann sinkt der Preis.

Wait until it's hailing, then the price will go down.

umtauschen
['ʊmtauʃən] *v*
to exchange

Ich möchte diese Euros umtauschen – die Farbe gefällt mir nicht.

I'd like to exchange these euros – I don't like the colour.

die Kasse
['kasə] *n*
the checkout, the cash desk

Verehrte Kunden, Kasse 17 schließt. Bitte benutzen Sie eine andere Kasse.

Customer information. Checkout 17 is closing. Please use another checkout.

der **Sport**
[spɔːt] *n*
the sport

Sport ist mein ganzes Leben.
Sport is my whole life.

rennen, laufen
['rɛnən], ['laufən] *v*
to run

Lauf schneller, der Pfarrer holt auf.

Run faster. The vicar's catching up.

das Rennen
['rɛnən] *n*
the race

Alina hängt bei jedem Rennen alle anderen ab.

Alina leaves everyone else trailing in every race.

trainieren
[trɛ'ni:rən] *v*
to train

Oleg trainiert für seine Rolle als Rocky VIII.

Oleg is training for his role as Rocky VIII.

der Spieler, die Spielerin
['ʃpi:le], ['ʃpi:lərɪn] *n*
the player

Gegen Spieler aus Fleisch und Blut tue ich mich leichter.

I find it easier against players made of flesh and blood.

fast, beinahe
[fast], ['baɪnaːə] *adv*
almost

Beinahe wäre ich Zweiter geworden.

I almost came second.

der Ball
[bal] *n*
the ball

Dirk macht mit dem Ball, was er will.

Dirk can do anything with the ball.

das Spiel, das Match
[ʃpiːl], [mɛtʃ] *n*
the game, the match

Das Spiel gegen die Mädels drohte persönlich zu werden.

The match against the girls was threatening to get personal.

springen
[ˈʃprɪŋən] *v*
to jump

Wenn Willi springt, sieht es so aus, als könne er fliegen.

When Willi jumps, it looks as if he can fly.

fangen
[ˈfaŋən] *v*
to catch

Der Löwe hatte eine überraschende Technik, um seine Beute zu fangen.

The lion had a surprising technique for catching its prey.

reiten
[ˈraɪtən] *v*
to ride

Ich wollte immer auf einem Elefanten reiten – nie wieder!

I've always wanted to ride an elephant – never again!

Ski laufen
[ˈʃiː laufən] *phrase*
to go skiing

Wir gehen immer zu Ostern Ski laufen.

We always go skiing at Easter.

die Wanderung
['vandərʊŋ] n
the hike

Ich bin jetzt doch froh, dass ich
bei der Wanderung dabei bin.

*Now I'm glad I came on this
hike after all.*

langsam
['laŋza:m] adj
slow

Ich bin nicht zu langsam.
Ihr seid zu ungeduldig.

*It's not me that's too slow.
It's you that's too impatient.*

schnell
[ʃnɛl] adj
fast

Martin muss wieder mit seinem
schnellen Boot angeben.

*Martin has to show off in his
fast boat again.*

werfen
['vɛrfən] v
to throw

Hendrik wirft sein achtes Tor!
Hendrik throws his eighth goal!

Fußball
['fu:sbal] n
football

Fußball ist auch vom
Spielfeldrand aus ganz schön.

*Football is also very nice
from the touchline.*

der Gegner,
die Gegnerin
['ge:gnɐ], ['ge:gnarɪn] n
the opponent

das Tor
['to:ɐ] n
the goal

schießen
['ʃi:sən] v
to shoot

der Wettkampf
['vɛtkampf] n
the competition

schwimmen
['ʃvɪmən] v
to swim

Ich nehme meine Ente immer mit,
wenn ich schwimmen gehe.

*I always take my duck
swimming with me.*

das Schwimmbad
['ʃvɪmba:t] n
the swimming pool

Hunde sind im Schwimmbad
eigentlich verboten.

*Dogs aren't really allowed in
the swimming pool.*

der Start
[ʃtart] *n*
the start

Er verlor schon beim Start zwei Sekunden.

He lost two seconds already at the start.

der Sieger, die Siegerin
[ˈziːɡə], [ˈziːɡərɪn] *n*
the winner

Der Sieger bekommt ein 24-teiliges Kaffeeservice.

The winner receives a 24-piece coffee service.

das Ziel
[tsiːl] *n*
the finish

Mit letzter Kraft erreichte Andreas das Ziel.

Andreas reached the finish on his last legs.

der Verlierer, die Verliererin
[fɛɐˈliːrə], [fɛɐˈliːrərɪn] *n*
the loser

Findet euch damit ab: Ihr seid die Verlierer.

You're the losers. Deal with it.

berühmt
[bəˈryːmt] *adj*
famous

Diese Nase ist seit über 3000 Jahren berühmt.

This nose has been famous for over 3000 years.

der Sieg
[ziːk] *n*
the victory

gewinnen
[ɡəˈvɪnən] *v*
to win

die Niederlage
[ˈniːdelaːɡə] *n*
the defeat

verlieren
[fɛɐˈliːrən] *v*
to lose

Schade, dass man nur vom Spielfeldrand aus fotografieren darf.

fotografieren
[fotoɡʁa'fiːʀən] *v*
to take pictures

Pity you're only allowed to take pictures from the touchline.

die Freizeit
['fʀaɪtsaɪt] *n*
the free time

Lass mich – ich kann in meiner Freizeit machen, was ich will.

Leave me alone – I can do what I like in my free time.

der Fotoapparat
['foːtoˌapaʀaːt] *n*
the camera

Mein Fotoapparat kann auch telefonieren.

My camera can also make phone calls.

das Motiv
[mo'tiːf] *n*
the subject

Ich hab' ein wirklich einzigartiges Motiv gefunden.

I've found a totally unique subject.

der Blitz
[blɪts] *n*
the flash

Ich liebe es, wenn die Blitze um mich herum aufleuchten.

I love it when the flashes are going off all around me.

spielen
['ʃpiːlən] v
spielen

Wenn Lara mit ihrer Katze spielt, ist sie gern ein bisschen gemein.

Lara likes to be a little bit mean when she plays with her cat.

das Spiel
[ʃpiːl] n
the game

Hätte ich nicht gedacht, dass ihr an so einem Spiel Spaß habt …

I wouldn't have thought you'd have enjoyed a game like that…

das Glück
[glʏk] n
the luck

Das Glück ließ Hannes auch diesmal nicht im Stich.

His luck hadn't deserted Hannes this time either.

der Würfel
['vʏrfəl] n
the dice

Blaue Würfel bringen mir immer Glück.

Blue dice always bring me luck.

das Pech
[pɛç] n
bad luck

Das war aber jetzt Pech. Probier's einfach noch mal.

That was just bad luck. Have another go.

einen Spaziergang machen

[aınən ʃpaˈtsiːɡaŋ maxən] *phrase*
to go for a walk

Emma trifft immer nette Leute, wenn sie **einen Spaziergang macht.**

Emma always meets nice people when she goes for a walk.

angeln
[ˈaŋəln] *v*
to fish

Wer **angeln** will, muss stillhalten können, Patrick.

If you want to fish, you have to be able to keep still, Patrick.

basteln
[ˈbastəln] *v*
to do handicrafts

Anna-Marie **bastelt** mit großem Ernst.

Anna-Marie takes doing handicrafts very seriously.

das Werkzeug
[ˈvɛʁktsɔʏk] *n*
the tool

Im Gebrauch von **Werkzeug** zeigt sich die Intelligenz.

The use of tools is a sign of intelligence.

das Taschenmesser
[ˈtaʃənmɛsɐ] *n*
the pocket knife

Er war so stolz: Sein **Taschenmesser** hatte 27 Werkzeuge.

He was so proud. His pocket knife had 27 tools.

die **Welt**

[vɛlt] *n*

the world

Meine Reise um die **Welt** war
schon nach zwei Wochen
beendet – hier wollte ich bleiben!

*My world tour ended after just
two weeks – I wanted to stay here!*

THE
WIDE
WORLD

die **Reise**

[ʀaɪzə] *n*

the journey

Luxus war uns auf unserer
Reise immer wichtig.

*Luxury always mattered to
us on our journey.*

das Reisebüro
['raɪzebyro:] *n*
the travel agency

Tut mir leid, unser Reisebüro ist auf Sibirien-Touren spezialisiert.

I'm terribly sorry, but our travel agency specializes in tours of Siberia.

die Landkarte
['lantkartə] *n*
the map

Ein Wunder: man berührt nur die Landkarte und schon geht's los!

It's incredible, you just touch the map and off you go!

der Urlaub, die Ferien
['u:elaup], [fe:ʀiən] *n*
the holiday

Ich! brauche! Urlaub!

I so need a holiday!

der Tourist, die Touristin
[tu'rɪst], [tu'rɪstɪn] *n*
the tourist

Das können nur Touristen sein.

They just have to be tourists.

Wenn du diese Reise buchst, storniere ich sie sofort wieder.

stornieren
[ʃtɔʀ'ni:ʀən] *v*
to cancel

If you book that trip, I'll cancel it straight away.

buchen
['bu:xən] *v*
to book

der Koffer
['kɔfe] *n*
the (suit)case

In dem Koffer fährt mein Bruder umsonst mit.

My brother's travelling with me free of charge in the suitcase.

packen
['pakən] *v*
to pack

Immer, wenn ich den Koffer packe, fehlt eine Socke.

Whenever I pack my case, there's always a sock missing.

reisen
['raɪzən] *v*
to travel

der Tourismus
[tu'rɪsmʊs] *n*
the tourism

touristisch
[tu'rɪstɪʃ] *adj*
tourist

das Gepäck
[gə'pɛk] *n*
the luggage

der Reisepass
['raɪzəpas] *n*
the passport

Hm, welcher Pass passt für meine nächste Mission?

Hmm, which passport should I go with for my next mission?

gültig
['gʊltɪç] *adj*
valid

das Hotel
[hoˈtɛl] *n*
the hotel

Schick: Hier im Hotel leiste ich mir immer den Zimmerservice.

Classy or what? I always splash out on room service when I'm staying at this hotel.

ankommen
['ankɔmən] *v*
ankommen

Kaum angekommen, ist Ferdinand schon wieder abgereist. Meinetwegen braucht er gar nicht mehr zurückzukommen.

Ferdinand left almost as soon as he arrived. He might as well not bother returning, for all I care.

abreisen
['apraɪzən] *v*
to leave

zurückkommen
[tsuˈrʏkkɔmən] *v*
to return

die **Jugendherberge**
[ju:gənthɛr'bɛrgə] n
the youth hostel

Eine Jugendherberge in seinem
Schloss hätte dem Herrn Grafen
gar nicht gefallen.

*The count would have been
appalled at the idea of a youth
hostel in his castle.*

ausgebucht
['ausgəbu:xt] adj
full

Alle Hotels sind ausgebucht.

All the hotels are full.

das **Zelt**
[tsɛlt] n
the tent

Hast du Idiot etwa den
Honig im Zelt gelassen?

*You idiot, you didn't
leave the honey in
the tent, did you?*

der **Schlafsack**
['ʃla:fzak] n
the sleeping bag

die **Rezeption**
[ʀetsɛp'tsjo:n] n
the reception

Bevor er verschwand, hinter-
ließ er ihr noch eine Nachricht
an der Rezeption.

*Before he took off, he left a
message for her with reception.*

der **Personal-
ausweis**
[pɛrzo'na:lausvais] n
the identity card

der **Campingplatz**
['kɛmpɪŋplats] n
the campsite

das **Doppelzimmer**
['dɔpəltsɪmə] n
the double room

das **Einzelzimmer**
['aintsəltsɪmə] n
the single room

die **Führung**
['fy:rʊŋ] *n*
the guided tour

Die Führung war in Rekordzeit beendet, danach gab's endlich Kaffee.

After finishing the guided tour in record time, they finally had some coffee.

führen
['fy:rən] *v*
to lead

besichtigen
[bə'zɪçtɪgən] *v*
to visit

Wir wollten noch das Schloss besichtigen – aber zu spät.

We wanted to visit the castle too, but we were too late.

die **Moschee**
[mɔ'ʃe:] *n*
the mosque

Die Hagia Sophia wurde nach 1453 zur Moschee umgebaut, ...

After 1453, the Hagia Sophia was converted into a mosque,...

die **Synagoge**
[zyna'go:gə] *n*
the synagogue

... die Jerusalem-Synagoge in Prag wurde 1906 vollendet, ...

...Prague's Jerusalem Synagogue was completed in 1906,...

die **Kirche**
['kɪrçə] *n*
the church

... die Kirche von Ronchamp wurde 1955 eingeweiht, ...

...the church at Ronchamp was consecrated in 1955,...

der **Dom,**
die **Kathedrale**
[do:m], [kathe'dra:lə] *n*
the cathedral

... am Kölner Dom hängen immer noch die Gerüste.

...Cologne Cathedral is still covered in scaffolding.

das **Museum**
[mu'ze:ʊm] *n*
the museum

Ist das noch ein Museum oder selbst schon Kunst?

Is this really still a museum, or is it a work of art in its own right?

der **Ausflug**
['ausfluːk] *n*
the trip

Der Ausflug ging nur in den Stadtpark, war aber super!

Although the trip was only to the town park, we had a really great time!

der **Turm**
[tʊrm] *n*
the tower

Jetzt ist der schiefe Turm doch noch umgekippt.

The leaning tower has finally fallen over.

der **Palast,**
das **Schloss**
[paˈlast], [ʃlɔs] *n*
the palace

Hier wohnst du, Felipe? Das ist ja ein Palast!

You live here, Felipe? It's a palace!

die **Burg**
[bʊrk] *n*
the castle

Auf dieser Burg hat vor 500 Jahren schon der Highlander gefroren.

The Highlander was already freezing to death in this castle 500 years ago.

COUNTRIES

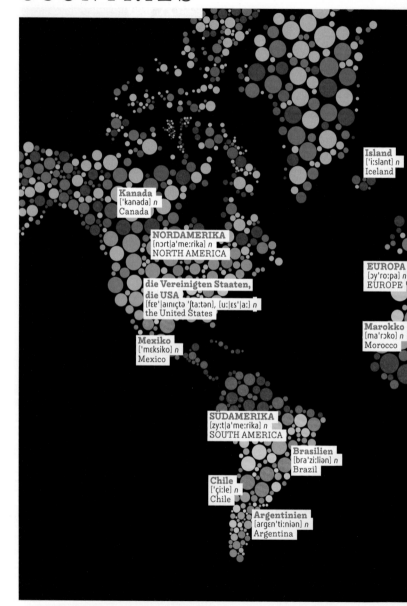

Island
['i:slant] *n*
Iceland

Kanada
['kanada] *n*
Canada

NORDAMERIKA
[nɔrt|a'me:rika] *n* ▶
NORTH AMERICA

EUROPA
[ɔy'ro:pa] *n*
EUROPE

**die Vereinigten Staaten,
die USA**
[fɛɛ'|aɪnɪçtə 'ʃta:tən], [u:|ɛs'|a:] *n*
the United States

Marokko
[ma'rɔko] *n*
Morocco

Mexiko
['mɛksiko] *n*
Mexico

SÜDAMERIKA
[zy:t|a'me:rika] *n*
SOUTH AMERICA

Brasilien
[bra'zi:liən] *n*
Brazil

Chile
['çi:le] *n*
Chile

Argentinien
[argɛn'ti:niən] *n*
Argentina

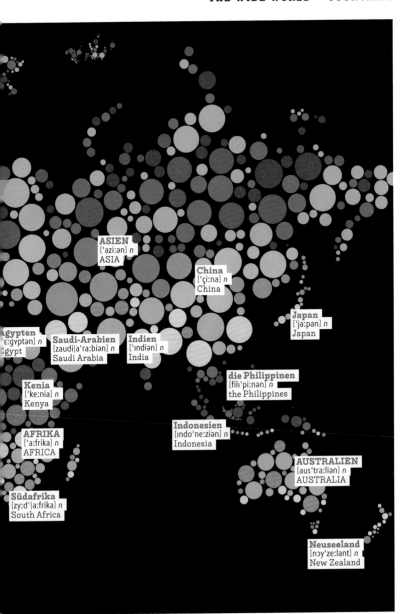

ASIEN
['azi:ən] *n*
ASIA

China
['çi:na] *n*
China

Japan
['ja:pan] *n*
Japan

Ägypten
[ɛ:gʏptən] *n*
Egypt

Saudi-Arabien
[zaudi|a'ra:biən] *n*
Saudi Arabia

Indien
['ɪndiən] *n*
India

die Philippinen
[fili'pi:nən] *n*
the Philippines

Kenia
['ke:nia] *n*
Kenya

Indonesien
[indo'ne:ziən] *n*
Indonesia

AFRIKA
['a:frika] *n*
AFRICA

AUSTRALIEN
[aus'tra:liən] *n*
AUSTRALIA

Südafrika
[zy:d'|a:frika] *n*
South Africa

Neuseeland
[nɔy'ze:lant] *n*
New Zealand

Finnland
['fɪnlant] *n*
Finland

Estland
['ɛstlant] *n*
Estonia

Russland
['rʊslant] *n*
Russia

Lettland
['lɛtlant] *n*
Latvia

8

Weißrussland
['vaɪsrʊslant] *n*
Belarus

Ukraine
[ukra'iːnə] *n*
Ukraine

9

Rumänien
[ru'mɛːniən] *n*
Romania

Bulgarien
[bʊl'gaːriən] *n*
Bulgaria

Türkei
[tʏr'kaɪ] *n*
Turkey

Griechenland
['griːçənlant] *n*
Greece

deutsch
[dɔʏtʃ] *adj*
German

Deutsches Frühstück: Kaffee,
Brötchen, Butter, Marmelade

A German breakfast:
coffee, bread rolls, butter
and jam

französisch
[fran'tsøːzɪʃ] *adj*
French

Französisches Frühstück:
Kaffee, Croissant

A French breakfast:
coffee and a croissant

englisch
['ɛŋlɪʃ] *adj*
English

Englisches Frühstück:
Speck, Eier, Bohnen

An English breakfast:
bacon, eggs and baked beans

spanisch
['ʃpaːnɪʃ] *adj*
Spanish

Spanisches Frühstück:
Churros, Trinkschokolade

A Spanish breakfast:
churros and drinking chocolate

norwegisch
['nɔrveːgɪʃ] *adj*
Norwegian

schwedisch
['ʃveːdɪʃ] *adj*
Swedish

irisch
['iːrɪʃ] *adj*
Irish

holländisch
['hɔlɛndɪʃ] *adj*
Dutch

belgisch
['bɛlgɪʃ] *adj*
Belgian

schweize-
risch
['ʃvaɪtsərɪʃ] *adj*
Swiss

italienisch
[ita'lieːnɪʃ] *adj*
Italian

griechisch
['griːçɪʃ] *adj*
Greek

portu-
giesisch
[pɔrtu'giːzɪʃ] *adj*
Portuguese

russisch
['rʊsɪʃ] *adj*
Russian

polnisch
['pɔlnɪʃ] *adj*
Polish

tschechisch
['tʃɛçɪʃ] *adj*
Czech

der **Verkehr**
[fɛɐ̯ˈkeːɐ̯] *n*
the traffic

Die größte Gefahr im Verkehr
sind Autos, die schneller fahren,
als ihr Fahrer denken kann.

*The greatest danger in traffic
is cars that go faster than their
drivers can think.*

das **Auto**
['auto] *n*
the car

Was denn? Du wolltest doch ein Auto zum 18. Geburtstag.

What's the matter? You said you wanted a car for your 18th birthday.

das **Motorrad**
[mo:'to:era:t] *n*
the motorbike

Als ich „Motorrad" hörte, hatte ich schon Angst, du wärst ein Rocker.

When I heard you mention your motorbike, I was worried you might be a rocker.

das **Taxi**
['taksi] *n*
the taxi

Taxi, Señor? Sie müssten nur etwas schieben helfen.

Taxi, señor? All you have to do is help give us a push-start.

das **Fahrrad**
['fa:era:t] *n*
the bicycle, the bike

Komm' ich mit meinem Fahrrad, springen die Leute zur Seite.

When I come along on my bike, people jump out of my way.

die **Strecke**
['ʃtrɛkə] *n*
the route

Die Strecke am Fluss entlang ist länger, dafür die schönere.

The route along the river is longer but more scenic.

Das ist ein Bibliotheks-ausweis, Sir, kein Führer-schein!

der **Fahrer**, die **Fahrerin**
['fa:re], ['fa:rərɪn] *n*
the driver

der **Führerschein**
['fy:reʃaɪn] *n*
the driving licence

This is a library card, sir, not a driving licence!

fahren
['fa:rən] *v*
to drive

die Tankstelle
['taŋkʃtɛlə] *n*
the filling station

Benzin verkauft er kaum an der Tankstelle, aber die Filmteams stehen Schlange.

He doesn't sell much petrol at his filling station, but he has film crews queuing up.

das Benzin
[bɛn'tsiːn] *n*
the petrol

der Diesel
['diːzəl] *n*
the diesel

die Straße
['ʃtraːsə] *n*
the street

Straßen sind die Lebensadern der Stadt – mit Infarktrisiko.

The streets are the arteries of the city – complete with the danger of a heart attack.

die (Land)Straße
['lantʃtʀaːsə] *n*
the road

Aus Gründen der Sicherheit sollten die Bäume an dieser Straße gefällt werden.

The trees along this road should be felled for safety reasons.

wenden
['vɛndən] *v*
to turn around, to make a U-turn

Wer wollte denn unbedingt wenden?

Who was it that insisted on turning around?

die Kreuzung
['kʀɔytsʊŋ] *n*
the crossroads

Wenn der Propeller jetzt aussetzt, stürzen wir direkt auf die Kreuzung.

If the propeller packed in now, we would crash right into the middle of the crossroads.

die Autobahn
['autobaːn] *n*
the motorway

So herrlich leer ist die Autobahn nur selten.

The motorway is very rarely as lovely and empty as this.

der **Reifen**
[raɪfən] *n*
the tyre

Muss man den Reifen vor dem
Aufpumpen nicht erst flicken?

*Aren't you supposed to patch
the tyre before you pump it up?*

der **Parkplatz**
['parkplats] *n*
the car park

parken
['parkən] *v*
to park

Auf dem ganzen Parkplatz war
kein einziger Platz mehr frei.

*There wasn't a single space
in the whole car park.*

die **Ampel**
['ampəl] *n*
the traffic
lights

Fast hätte ich die
Ampel übersehen.

*I almost didn't see the
traffic lights.*

(an)halten
['(an)haltən] *v*
to stop

verbrauchen
[fɛɐ̯ˈbrauxən] *v*
to use

Daddy hat ihn mir geschenkt,
keine Ahnung, was er
verbraucht.

*Daddy gave it to me as a
present, I haven't a clue how
much fuel it uses.*

der **Gehweg**
['geːveːk] *n*
the pavement

Dein holder Gang veredelt selbst
den langweiligsten Gehweg.

*You make even the dullest pave-
ment look good when you walk
along it with your graceful gait.*

die Brücke
['brʏkə] *n*
the bridge

Ohne die Brücke ging es tatsächlich schneller.

It was actually quicker without the bridge.

die Eisenbahn
['aɪzənbaːn] *n*
the railway

So begann die Karriere meines Vaters bei der Eisenbahn.

And that was how my dad's career on the railways began.

die Fahrkarte
['faːekaʁtə] *n*
the ticket

Seine Sammlung alter Fahrkarten ist heute richtig was wert.

His collection of old tickets is now worth a fortune.

verpassen
[fɛɐ'pasən] *v*
to miss

Verdammt! Zug verpasst … der nächste fährt in drei Tagen.

Damn! I missed the train…and the next one isn't for three days.

der Fahrplan
['faːeplaːn] *n*
the timetable

Du liest den Fahrplan? Hast du keine App?

What are you reading the timetable for? Haven't you got an app?

die Ankunft
['ankʊnft] *n*
the arrival

Genau so habe ich mir meine Ankunft vorgestellt.

This was exactly how I imagined my arrival.

die Abfahrt
['apfaːet] *n*
the departure

Die Abfahrt des Zuges verzögert sich um wenige Minuten.

The train's departure will be delayed by a few minutes.

der Bahnhof
['baːnhoːf] *n*
the station

This is a passenger announcement.
This station will be closing for renovation. The last train will depart from platform 13. We regret to announce that the on-board air-conditioning is out of order. Thank you for your understanding.

Verehrte Fahrgäste. Wegen Umbauarbeiten wird dieser Bahnhof gesperrt. Der letzte Zug fährt von Gleis 13. Die Klimaanlage im Zug ist leider ausgefallen. Wir danken Ihnen für Ihr Verständnis.

der Zug
[tsuːk] *n*
the train

der Bahnsteig, das Gleis
['baːnʃtaɪk], [glaɪs] *n*
the platform

der (Sitz)Platz
[('zɪts)plats] *n*
the seat

Komm rein, Liebling, es ist ein Platz frei geworden.

Come in, dear, there's a free seat now.

direkt
[diˈrɛkt] *adj*
direct

Ich habe eine direkte Verbindung bis ans Meer.

I have a direct connection to the seaside.

der Anschluss
['anʃlʊs] *n*
the connection

umsteigen
['ʊmʃtaɪgən] *v*
to change trains

das Abteil
[apˈtaɪl] *n*
the compartment

der Schaffner, die Schaffnerin
['ʃafnɐ], ['ʃafnərɪn] *n*
the conductor

die Straßenbahn
['ʃtraːsənbaːn] *n*
the tram

In Hongkong sind die Straßenbahnen doppelstöckig.

In Hong Kong, they have double-decker trams.

die Haltestelle
['haltaʃtɛlə] *n*
the (bus) stop

Wie gut, dass diese Haltestelle wetterfest ist.

Thank God this bus stop is weatherproof.

der Bus
[bus] *n*
the bus

Auf dem Dach des Busses war die Luft deutlich besser.

The air was much fresher on the roof of the bus.

die Zeitkarte
['tsaɪtkarta] *n*
the season ticket

die Fluggesellschaf
['fluːkgəzelʃaft] *n*
the airline

der Flugplan
['fluːkplaːn] *n*
the schedule

die U-Bahn
['uːbaːn] *n*
the underground, the subway

Ich bin ganz froh, dass die U-Bahn nicht immer im Untergrund fährt.

I'm really glad the underground doesn't always run underground.

der **Flughafen**
['flu:kha:fən] n
the airport

Am Flughafen darf man keinen Koffer rumstehen lassen, haben sie durchgesagt.

There was an announcement saying you shouldn't leave your baggage unattended at the airport.

der **Flug**
[flu:k] n
the flight

Typisch! Nur mein Flug hat mal wieder Verspätung.

Typical! My flight is the only one that's delayed again.

starten
['ʃtartən] v
to take off

Ihre Band startete wie eine Rakete.

Their band took off like a rocket.

fliegen
['fli:gən] v
to fly

Aaron und Henry flogen die kühnsten Loopings über der Savanne.

Aaron and Henry flew some death-defying loop-the-loops over the savannah.

landen
['landən] v
to land

Bitte warten Sie mit dem Applaus, bis die Maschine gelandet ist.

Please don't start clapping until the plane has actually landed.

das **Flugzeug**
['flu:ktsɔyk] n
the plane

Im Flugzeug spielt der Pilot am liebsten an den vielen Knöpfchen herum.

When he's on board the plane, there's nothing the pilot likes better than playing with all the little buttons.

das Schiff
[ʃɪf] *n*
the ship

Dieses Schiff ist
unsinkbar.

*This ship
is unsinkable.*

sinken
['zɪŋkən] *v*
to sink

das Boot
[boːt] *n*
the boat

In seinem Boot fühlte er sich
wie bei Miami Vice.

*His boat made him feel like
he was in Miami Vice.*

der Hafen
['haːfən] *n*
the port

die Fähre
['fɛːrə] *n*
the ferry

Der Brücke traue ich nicht,
ich nehme lieber die Fähre.

*I don't trust the bridge, I think
I'll take the ferry instead.*

überleben
[y:be'le:bən] *v*
to survive

Schutzanzüge können durchaus
helfen zu überleben.

*Protective suits can definitely
help you survive.*

zusammenstoßen
[tsu'zamənʃto:sən] *v*
to crash, to collide

Du Riesenrindvieh! Wir wären
um ein Haar zusammengestoßen!

*You stupid idiot! We were a hair's
breadth away from crashing there!*

plötzlich
['plœtsliç] *adv*
suddenly

Anton hatte plötzlich eine
super Idee.

*Anton suddenly had a
brilliant idea.*

der Zusammenstoß
[tsu'zamənʃto:s] *n*
the crash

abstürzen
['apʃtʏrtsən] *v*
to crash, to fall
down

retten
['rɛtən] *v*
to rescue

der Unfall
['ʊnfal] *n*
the accident

Das hab' ich nicht absichtlich
gemacht, das war ein Unfall.

*I didn't do it on purpose,
it was an accident.*

ANIMALS & PLANTS

das **Tier**

[tiːe] *n*

the animal

Nein Mia, die können wir nicht mitnehmen – **Tiere** gehören nicht in die Wohnung!

No Mia, we can't take them home – animals don't belong in the house!

die **Kuh**
[ku:] *n*
the cow

Dieses Kalb säuft mir die ganze Milch meiner Kuh weg!

That calf is drinking up all my cow's milk!

das **Kalb**
[kalp] *n*
the calf

das **Schwein**
[ʃvaɪn] *n*
the pig, the hog

Im Leben muss man eben manchmal ein Schwein sein.

Sometimes you should live life like a pig.

das **Pferd**
['pfeːet] *n*
the horse

Ich hab' heute wieder aufs falsche Pferd gesetzt.

I bet on the wrong horse again today.

der **Hund**
[hʊnt] *n*
the dog

Mein Hund kommt sofort, wenn ich die Dose öffne.

My dog comes running as soon as I open the tin.

die **Ziege**
['tsiːɡə] *n*
the goat

Ziegen, die auf Bäume klettern? Glaub' ich nicht!

Goats that climb up trees? Pull the other one!

das **Schaf**
[ʃaːf] *n*
the sheep

Die Schafe starrten mich böse an, als ich die Kamera zückte.

The sheep stared at me angrily when I got my camera out.

die **Wolle**
['vɔlə] *n*
the wool

Die Wolle hat auch noch für ein prima Mützchen gereicht. Danke Mami!

There was enough wool left over to make a lovely little hat. Thank you so much, Mummy!

die Maus
[maus] *n*
the mouse

die Katze
['katsə] *n*
the cat

Noch fühlt sich die Maus sicher, aber die Katze hat alle Zeit der Welt …

The mouse still feels safe, but the cat has all the time in the world…

der Vogel
['foːgəl] *n*
the bird

Vögel frieren nicht so schnell an den Füßen wie Menschen.

Birds' feet don't freeze as quickly as people's.

der Fisch
['fɪʃ] *n*
the fish

Den Fisch von meinem Sushi mag ich am liebsten gut durchgebraten.

I prefer the fish in my sushi to be well fried.

das Huhn
[huːn] *n*
the chicken

Sag mal, Mama, müssen alle Hühner nach Kentucky?

Mummy, do all chickens have to go to Kentucky?

das Gras
[graːs] *n*
the grass

Das Gras unter den Füßen spüren – endlich ist Sommer!

I can feel the grass under my feet again – it's summer at last!

die Rose
['roːzə] *n*
the rose

Die Nummer mit der Rose haben wir aus einem Film geklaut.

We pinched the number with the rose from a film.

die Blume
['bluːmə] *n*
the flower

Das Geschäft mit Blumen floriert.

The flower business is flourishing.

das Blatt
[blat] *n*
the leaf

der Baum
[baum] *n*
the tree

Auf diesen Baum bin ich
schon als Mädchen
geklettert. Aber da waren
wir beide noch kleiner.

*I used to climb up this tree
when I was a girl. But we were
both a lot smaller back then.*

der Zweig, der Ast
[tsvaɪk], [ast] *n*
the branch

das Holz
[hɔlts] *n*
the wood

Mitten im Wald bauten wir ein
Baumhaus aus Holz.

*We built a treehouse out of
wood in the middle of the forest.*

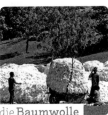

die Baumwolle
['baumvɔlə] *n*
the cotton

Die Baumwolle dürfte für ein
paar T-Shirts reichen.

*There should be enough cotton
for a couple of T-shirts.*

das Getreide
[ɡəˈtraɪdə] *n*
the grain

Die Deutschen backen aus
den verschiedensten Arten
von Getreide ihr Brot.

*The Germans make their
bread from all sorts of
different grains.*

wachsen
['vaksən] *v*
to grow

die Pflanze
['pflantsə] *n*
the plant

Seit hier Pflanzen wachsen,
verkaufe ich kaum mehr Luftballons.

*I've hardly sold any balloons since
the plants started growing here.*

THE ENVIRONMENT

die **Landschaft**
['lantʃaft] *n*
the landscape

Wenn wir den Staudamm nach Norden verlegen, bleibt noch ein bisschen Landschaft übrig.

If we move the dam to the north, some of the landscape will still be left unspoilt.

die Umwelt
['ʊmvɛlt] *n*
the environment

Die Umwelt interessiert umso
weniger, je weiter man weg ist.

*The further removed people
are from the environment,
the less they are interested in it.*

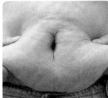

das Gebiet, die Zone
[gə'biːt], ['tsoːnə] *n*
the area

Meine wirkliche Problemzone
ist mein Mund.

*My real problem area is my
mouth.*

die Region
[re'gioːn] *n*
the region

Ich probiere immer alle
Spezialitäten der Region.

*I always try all the region's
specialities.*

regional
[regio'naːl] *adj*
regional

Wir haben gern etwas
regionales Kolorit beim
Waldspaziergang.

*We like to bring some regional
colour to our walks in the woods.*

der Kontinent
['kɔntinɛnt] *n*
the continent

Nach den Wikingern entdeckte
auch Kolumbus den Kontinent.

*After the Vikings, Columbus also
discovered the continent.*

das Land
[lant] *n*
**the land,
the country**

Das Leben ist hart auf
dem Land.

Life in the country is hard.

der Grund,
der Boden
[grʊnt], ['boːdən] *n*
the ground

Kaum berührt das Flugzeug den
Grund, schon hängt Mr. Wichtig
am Telefon.

*The second plane touches
the ground, Mr Important is
already on his phone.*

der (Erd)Boden
['boːdən], ['(eːet)boːdən] *n*
the soil

Glaubst du, mein Gummi-
bärchenbaum wächst auf
diesem Boden?

*Do you think my gummi bear
tree will grow in this soil?*

das Eisen
['aɪzən] *n*
the iron

Sie brauchen 7300 Tonnen Eisen? So ein Zufall, die haben wir hier rumstehen ...

You need 7,300 tonnes of iron? What a coincidence, we just happen to have that much standing around here...

das Gas
[gaːs] *n*
the gas

Falscher Alarm: Es war kein Gas, sondern Lisas Zwiebelsuppe.

False alarm – it wasn't gas, it was Lisa's onion soup.

das (Erd)Öl
[(eːet)øːl] *n*
the (crude) oil

Wie, ihr verbrennt das ganze schöne Erdöl einfach?

What? You're just burning all that lovely oil?

das Metall
[meˈtal] *n*
the metal

Metall verändert seine Form unter hohem Druck.

Metal changes its shape at high pressures.

das Gold
[gɔlt] *n*
the gold

Wie findste meinen neuen Goldzahn?

What do you think of my new gold tooth?

das Silber
['zɪlbe] *n*
the silver

Ursprünglich hatte das Silberbesteck mal 96 Teile.

Originally, this set of silver cutlery had 96 pieces.

das **Erdbeben**
['e:etbe:bən] *n*
the earthquake

Nein, kein durchgeknallter Architekt, nur ein Erdbeben.

No, not a whacky architect, just an earthquake.

die **Wüste**
['vy:stə] *n*
the desert

Ein Pool mitten in der Wüste – herrlich!

How wonderful, a swimming pool in the middle of the desert!

der **Gipfel**
['gɪpfəl] *n*
the peak

der **Berg**
[bɛrk] *n*
the mountain

Der Berg ruft, aber ich hör' weg.

The mountain is calling, but I'm not listening.

der **Wald**
[valt] *n*
the forest

der **Fluss**
[flʊs] *n*
the river

der **Weg**
[ve:k] *n*
the path

Du immer mit deinen Abkürzungen. Dieser Weg führt ins Nichts!

You and your shortcuts. This path doesn't go anywhere!

der **Hügel**
['hy:gəl] *n*
the hill

In diesem Haus auf dem Hügel möchte ich alt werden.

I'd like to grow old in this house on the hill.

der See
[zeː] *n*
the lake

Der Elch steigt aus dem See, und ich erwarte ihn am Ufer.

As the moose comes out of the lake, I wait for him on the bank.

das Ufer
[ˈuːfɐ] *n*
the bank

die Küste
[ˈkʏstə] *n*
the coast

Das Ferienhaus an der Küste hatte überhaupt keinen Strand.

The holiday home was on the coast, but nowhere near a beach.

die Insel
[ˈɪnzəl] *n*
the island

Hey Mädels, ich hab' die Insel die ganze Woche gemietet.

Hey ladies, I've rented the island out for the whole week.

der Strand
[ʃtrant] *n*
the beach

Als wir zum Strand kamen, gab es nur noch Stehplätze.

By the time we got to the beach, it was standing room only.

das Wasser
[ˈvasɐ] *n*
the water

Willst du es nicht doch mal im Wasser probieren?

Don't you think it's time you tried it out on the water?

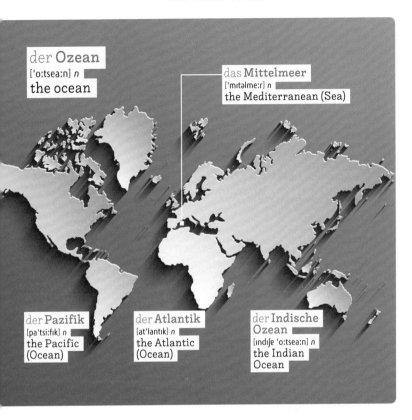

der **Ozean**
[ˈoːtseaːn] *n*
the ocean

das **Mittelmeer**
[ˈmɪtəlmeːr] *n*
the Mediterranean (Sea)

der **Pazifik**
[paˈtsiːfɪk] *n*
the Pacific
(Ocean)

der **Atlantik**
[atˈlantɪk] *n*
the Atlantic
(Ocean)

der **Indische
Ozean**
[ɪndɪʃe ˈoːtseaːn] *n*
the Indian
Ocean

die **Welle**
[ˈvɛlə] *n*
the wave

Wir müssen noch durch
diese Welle, dann
haben wir es geschafft.

*We just need to get
through this one last
wave, then we'll
have made it.*

das **Meer**
[ˈmeːɐ] *n*
the sea

Ohne Stau durchs Meer auf dem
Weg zum Schildkrötentreffen.

*No traffic hold-ups on my
way through the sea to the
turtle convention.*

das **Wetter**
['vɛtɐ] *n*
the weather

Es gibt kein schlechtes Wetter, nur falsche Kleidung.

There's no such thing as bad weather, just the wrong clothes.

das **Klima**
['kliːma] *n*
the climate

Das Klima verändert sich, mein Kind.

The climate is changing, my child.

die **Temperatur**
[tɛmpəra'tuːɐ] *n*
the temperature

Bei der richtigen Temperatur schneide ich Glas mit der Schere.

If the temperature is right, I can cut glass with a pair of scissors.

sonnig
[ˈzɔnɪç] *adj*
sunny

An sonnigen Tagen bevorzuge ich alkoholfreie Drinks.

I prefer alcohol-free drinks on sunny days.

normal
[nɔrˈmaːl] *adj*
normal

Schnee zu Ostern ist schon fast normal geworden.

Nowadays, it's almost normal for it to snow at Easter.

kühl
[kyːl] *adj*
cool

Wer die Wohnung kühl haben will, muss die Umwelt heizen.

Keeping your flat cool means heating up the environment.

heiß
[haɪs] *adj*
hot

kalt
[kalt] *adj*
cold

warm
[ˈvarm] *adj*
warm

die **Wolke**
[ˈvɔlkə] *n*
the cloud

Hubraum schön und gut, aber das Wichtigste war ihm die schicke Wolke.

The powerful engine was all well and good, but the most important thing for him was the cool dust cloud.

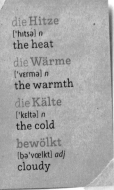

die **Hitze**
[ˈhɪtsə] *n*
the heat

die **Wärme**
[ˈvɛrmə] *n*
the warmth

die **Kälte**
[ˈkɛltə] *n*
the cold

bewölkt
[bəˈvœlkt] *adj*
cloudy

trocken
['trɔkən] *adj*
dry

Richtig **trocken** wird es nur von Hand.

The only way to get it properly dry is by hand.

der Wind
[vɪnt] *n*
the wind

wehen, blasen
['ve:ən], ['bla:zən] *v*
to blow

Wenn der **Wind** so heftig **weht**, freut sich mein Friseur.

My hairdresser's always happy when the wind blows so strongly.

nass
[nas] *adj*
wet

Auch wenn ich **nass** werde, ich bleibe hier, bis Don Silvio mich braucht.

I don't care if I get wet, I'm staying here till Don Silvio needs me.

der Sturm
[ʃtʊrm] *n*
the storm

Ihr Memmen, dieses laue Lüftchen nennt ihr einen **Sturm**?

Call this a storm? It's no more than a gentle breeze, you wimps!

der Regen
['re:gən] *n*
the rain

Im **Regen** habe ich am meisten Spaß – meine Eltern weniger.

I always have a great time in the rain – unlike my parents.

der Blitz
[blɪts] *n*
the lightning

Blitze machen auch vor Kirchen nicht Halt.

Lightning doesn't even spare churches.

das Gewitter
[gə'vɪtɐ] *n*
the thunderstorm

der Nebel
['ne:bəl] *n*
the fog

Der **Nebel** hat das Industrie-gebiet gnädig zugedeckt.

Fortunately, the fog has completely covered over the industrial estate.

schneien
['ʃnaɪən] *v*
to snow

Nur Kinder freuen sich, wenn es schneit.

Only children are happy when it snows.

das **Feuer**
[fɔɰe] *n*
the fire

Im Feuer verbrannte auch meine ganze Comicsammlung.

My entire comic collection also burned in the fire.

(ver)brennen
['brɛnən], [fɛɛ'brɛnən] *v*
to burn

das **Eis**
[aɪs] *n*
the ice

Bleiben wir lieber drin, der Balkon ist voll Eis.

We'd better stay inside, the balcony's covered in ice.

die Über-schwemmung
[y:be'ʃvɛmʊŋ] *n*
the flood

Ist das noch eine Pfütze oder schon eine Überschwemmung?

Would you still call this a puddle, or does it count as a flood now?

neblig
['ne:blɪç] *adj*
foggy

der Schnee
[ʃne:] *n*
the snow

regnen
['re:gnən] *v*
to rain

THE COSMOS

das **All**,
das **Universum**
[al], [uniˈvɛrzʊm] *n*
the universe

Zwei Dinge sind unendlich,
das Universum und die
menschliche Dummheit …

*Two things are infinite,
the universe and human
stupidity…*

der **Weltraum**
[ˈvɛltraum] *n*
space

der Himmel
['hɪməl] *n*
the sky

Flugzeuge gehören in den Himmel, nicht an den Strand.

Planes belong in the sky, not on the beach.

der Mond
[moːnt] *n*
the moon

die Erde
['eːedə] *n*
the earth

Von der Erde zum Mond braucht das Licht knapp 1,5 Sekunden.

It takes light just under 1.5 seconds to travel from the earth to the moon.

die Sonne
['zɔnə] *n*
the sun

Die Sonne hat manchmal einen besonderen Sinn für Dramatik.

Sometimes the sun seems to have a real sense of drama.

die Luft
[lʊft] *n*
the air

Seltsames Tier: Es trägt seine Luft auf dem Rücken.

What a funny creature, it carries its air on its back.

der Stern
[ʃtern] *n*
the star

Für jeden echten Star gibt es hier einen Stern.

Every true star has their own star here.

der Astronaut, die Astronautin
[astro'naut], [astro'nautɪn], *n*
the astronaut

Nicht jeder Astronaut heißt Major Tom.

Not every astronaut is called Major Tom.

der Satellit
[zatɛ'liːt] *n*
the satellite

Der Todesstrahl des Satelliten richtete sich auf Bad Aibling.

The satellite's death ray was aimed at Bad Aibling.

die **Zeit**

[tsaɪt] *n*

the time

Eine Sonnenfinsternis sieht man nur für kurze **Zeit**.

You only see an eclipse of the sun for a short time.

SPACE & TIME

das **Jahr**
['jaːɐ] *n*
the year

Im Jahr des Drachen, heißt es,
werden große Männer geboren.

*They say that great men are
born in the year of the dragon.*

der **Januar**
['janua:ɐ] n
January

der **Februar**
['fe:brua:ɐ] n
February

der **März**
[mɛrts] n
March

der **April**
[a'prɪl] n
April

der **Mai**
['maɪ] n
May

der **Juni**
['ju:ni] n
June

der **Juli**
['ju:li] n
July

der **August**
[au'gʊst] n
August

der **September**
[zɛp'tɛmbɐ] n
September

der **Oktober**
[ɔk'to:bɐ] n
October

der **November**
[no:'vɛmbɐ] n
November

der **Dezember**
[de'tsɛmbɐ] n
December

der **Frühling**
['fry:lɪŋ] *n*
the spring

der **Sommer**
['zɔmɐ] *n*
the summer

der **Herbst**
[hɛrpst] *n*
the autumn

der **Winter**
[wɪntɐ] *n*
the winter

In German, the names of the seasons are usually preceeded by *im*: *im Frühling, im Sommer, im Herbst, im Winter.*

die **Jahreszeit**, die **Saison**
['jaːʁəstsaɪt], [zɛ'zõ:] *n*
the season

In der Ski-Saison haben die Ärzte Hochkonjunktur.

The skiing season is the busiest time of year for doctors.

der **Monat**
['moːnat] *n*
the month

Der Monat August ist für viele gleichbedeutend mit Ferien.

For many people, the month of August is synonymous with holidays.

die Woche
['vɔxə] *n*
the week

Heinz richtet seine Medikamente
für die Woche her.

*Heinz is sorting out his meds for
the week.*

das Wochenende
['vɔxən|əndə] *n*
the weekend

Am Wochenende habe ich
Manu endlich wiedergesehen.

*I finally saw Manu again at
the weekend.*

der Werktag
['vɛrktaːk] *n*
the working day

Die Vertragsunterzeichnung war
kein Werktag wie jeder andere.

*The day we signed the contract
wasn't just any old working day.*

der Montag
['moːntaːk] *n*
Monday

der Dienstag
['diːnstaːk] *n*
Tuesday

der Mittwoch
['mɪtvɔx] *n*
Wednesday

der Donnerstag
['dɔnɐstaːk] *n*
Thursday

der Freitag
['fraɪtaːk] *n*
Friday

der Samstag
['zamstaːk] *n*
Saturday

der Sonntag
['zɔntaːk] *n*
Sunday

Heiligabend
['haɪlɪç'|aːbənt] n
Christmas Eve

Nein Sophie, die Kugeln bleiben bis nach Heiligabend dran.

No Sophie, the baubles have to stay on till Christmas Eve is over.

Weihnachten
['vaɪhnaxtən] n
Christmas

Dieses Jahr verbringen wir Weihnachten am Strand.

This year we're having Christmas on the beach.

der Neujahrstag
['nɔyjaːestaːk] n
New Year's Day

Schon am Neujahrstag waren alle guten Vorsätze vergessen.

It was only New Year's Day and all the resolutions had already been forgotten.

Silvester
[zɪl'vəste] n
New Year's Eve

Ohne Feuerwerk kann ich mir Silvester gar nicht vorstellen.

I simply can't imagine New Year's Eve without the fireworks.

der **Karneval**
['karnəval] *n*
the carnival

Im diesjährigen Karneval hatte Marisa ihren großen Auftritt mit den Schmetterlingen.

Marisa had her big appearance with the butterflies at this year's carnival.

der **Karfreitag**
[kaːeˈfʀaitaːk] *n*
Good Friday

Am Karfreitag gibt es überall auf der Welt Prozessionen.

On Good Friday there are processions all over the world.

Ostern
['oːsten] *n*
Easter

Glaubst du wirklich, dass zu Ostern ein Hase die Eier bringt?

Do you really believe that a bunny brings the eggs at Easter?

Pfingsten
['wɪtsn] *n*
Whitsun

An Pfingsten kommt der Heilige Geist herab.

The Holy Ghost descends at Whitsun.

der **Tag**
[ta:k] *n*
the day

Das war der Tag, als Oskar
Fahrrad fahren gelernt hat.

*This was the day Oskar
learned to ride a bike.*

täglich
['tɛːklɪç] *adj*
daily

Unsere tägliche Fahrt aufs Festland in die Schule war echt lustig.

Our daily trip to school on the mainland was great fun.

die Mitternacht
['mɪtɐnaxt] *n*
midnight

Um Mitternacht erschien der Geist der toten Stieftochter.

The ghost of the dead stepdaughter appeared at midnight.

der Nachmittag
['naːxmɪtaːk] *n*
the afternoon

Meine Nachmittage verbringe ich meist auf dem Golfplatz.

I generally spend my afternoons on the golf course.

In German, a day can be divided up into the following: morgens, vormittags (in the morning), mittags (at noon), nachmittags (in the afternoon), abends (in the evening), nachts (at night).

der Morgen
['mɔrgən] *n*
the morning

der Mittag
['mɪtaːk] *n*
the noon

der Abend
['aːbənt] *n*
the evening

die Nacht
[naxt] *n*
the night

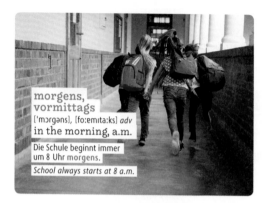

morgens, vormittags
['mɔrgəns], [fo:emita:ks] *adv*
in the morning, a.m.

Die Schule beginnt immer um 8 Uhr morgens.

School always starts at 8 a.m.

die **Sekunde**
[ze'kʊndə] *n*
the second

Es sind noch zwei Sekunden bis zwölf.

There are still two seconds to go until twelve o'clock.

nachmittags
['na:xmɪtaks] *adv*
in the afternoon, p.m.

Die Schule endet heute erst um halb vier nachmittags.

We only finish school at 3.30 p.m. today.

die **Minute**
[mi'nu:tə] *n*
the minute

Tiefkühlspinat braucht acht Minuten in meiner Mikrowelle.

Frozen spinach takes eight minutes in my microwave.

die **Stunde**
['ʃtʊndə] *n*
the hour

So eine Oper kann viele Stunden dauern. Sehr viele Stunden …

Operas like these can go on for hours. Hours and hours…

um
[ʊm] *prep*
at

Um ein Uhr nachts ist auf den Straßen noch was los.

The streets are still full of life at one o'clock in the morning.

... **Uhr**
['u:ɐ] *adv*
... o'clock

Bis zwei Uhr nachts liest Leo heimlich „Huckleberry Finn".

Leo secretly reads "Huckleberry Finn" until two o'clock in the morning.

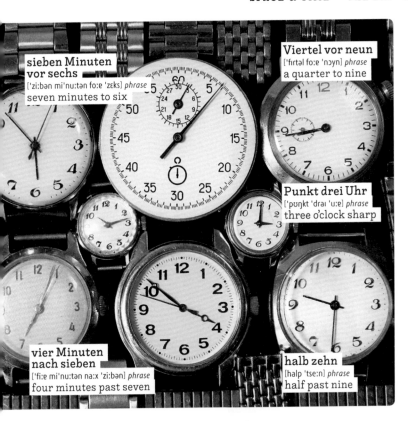

sieben Minuten vor sechs
['ziːbən miˈnuːtən foːɐ 'zɛks] *phrase*
seven minutes to six

Viertel vor neun
['fɪrtəl foːɐ 'nɔyn] *phrase*
a quarter to nine

Punkt drei Uhr
['pʊŋkt 'draɪ 'uːɐ] *phrase*
three o'clock sharp

vier Minuten nach sieben
['fiːɐ miˈnuːtən naːx 'ziːbən] *phrase*
four minutes past seven

halb zehn
[halp 'tseːn] *phrase*
half past nine

Wie spät ist es?
[viː 'ʃpɛːt ɪst ɛs] *phrase*
What time is it?

Ich habe keine Ahnung, **wie spät es ist.**

I have no idea what time it is.

die **Viertelstunde**
[fɪrtəlˈʃtʊndə] *n*
the quarter of an hour

Eine Viertelstunde hat sie gesagt, und das war vor einer halben Stunde …

She said a quarter of an hour and that was half an hour ago…

die **halbe Stunde**
[halbə 'ʃtʊndə] *n*
half an hour

heute

['hɔytə] *adv*

today

Heute erwische ich die
perfekte Welle.

*Today I'm going to catch
the perfect wave.*

gestern
['gɛstən] *adv*
yesterday

Hätte ich gestern nur das Wasser gewechselt.

If only I'd changed the water yesterday.

morgen
['mɔrgən] *adv*
tomorrow

Morgen müsste die Blüte ganz aufgegangen sein.

The flower should be completely open tomorrow.

während
['vɛːrənt] *prep*
during

Während seiner Einradnummer jongliert Tom mit fünf Bällen.

Tom juggles five balls during his monocycle act.

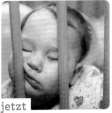

jetzt
[jɛtst] *adv*
now

Jetzt ist er schließlich eingeschlafen.

He's finally gone to sleep now.

vor
[foːɐ] *adv*
ago

Das war vor 85 Jahren, als meine Großeltern heirateten.

This was 85 years ago, when my grandparents got married.

das Datum
[daːtʊm] *n*
the date

Eriks Uhr zeigt sogar das richtige Datum an.

Erik's watch even shows the right date.

der Moment
[moˈmɛnt] *n*
the moment

Sie passte genau den richtigen Moment ab.

She waited for exactly the right moment.

wann
[van] *adv*
when

Wann wollte Papa mich abholen?

When was Dad supposed to be picking me up?

zuerst
[tsu'|e:est] *adv*
first

danach, dann
[da'na:x], [dan] *adv*
then

zuletzt
[tsu'lɛtst] *adv*
last

früh
[fry:] *adv*
early

Wenn ich früh genug da bin,
habe ich den See ganz für mich.

If I get there early enough,
I have the whole lake to myself.

spät
[ʃpɛ:t] *adv*
late

Spät am Abend beginnt die
Stadt zu leuchten.

The city starts to glow late
in the evening.

rechtzeitig
['rɛçtsaɪtɪç] *adv*
in time

Zum Glück ist der Ring noch
rechtzeitig geliefert worden.

Luckily, the ring was delivered
in time.

plötzlich
['plœtslɪç] *adv*
suddenly

Plötzlich knallte es, und eine
Lawine raste auf uns zu.

Suddenly there was a bang
and an avalanche came
racing towards us.

sofort
[zo'fɔrt] *adv*
immediately,
at once

Der Notarzt war sofort da.

The emergency doctor came
at once.

beginnen, anfangen
[bə'gɪnən], ['anfaŋən] v
to begin, to start

Die Ferien fangen ja gut an …

Well, the holidays are starting well…

(be)enden
[(bə)'ɛndən] v
to end

Der Western endete wie üblich.

The western ended in the usual manner.

bald
[balt] adv
soon

Bald ist es soweit, und dann können wir nicht mehr abends weggehen.

It'll soon be here and then we can forget about going out in the evenings.

bevor, vor
[bə'foːɐ], [foːɐ] prep
before

Zieh gefälligst deine Stiefel aus, bevor du reinkommst.

Kindly take your boots off before you come in.

nach
[naːx] prep
after

Nach dem Essen räumt jeder seinen Teller ab, sonst gibt es keinen Nachtisch.

Everyone has to clear their own plate away after dinner or there won't be any dessert.

anhalten, stoppen
['anhaltən], ['ʃtɔpən] v
to stop

Schnell, halt die Maschine an!

Quick, stop the machine!

sobald
[zoˈbalt] *conj*
as soon as

Sobald der Bogen fertig ist, kommt die Fahrbahn drüber.

As soon as the arch is ready, the roadway comes on top.

seit
[zaɪt] *prep*
since, for

Seit der Steinzeit versucht der Mensch, sich weiterzubilden.

Ever since the Stone Age, man has been trying to increase his learning.

bis
[bɪs] *prep*
until

Auch wenn kein Zug zu sehen ist: Wir müssen warten, bis die Schranke hoch geht.

Even if there's no train in sight, we still have to wait until the barrier goes up.

schon
[ʃoːn] *adv*
already

Sehe ich wirklich schon so alt aus?

Do I really look so old already?

dauern
[ˈdauen] *v*
to take, to last

Er hat die Zeitung dabei – das wird dauern.

He's got the newspaper in there – this could take a while.

meistens, normalerweise
[ˈmaɪstəns], [ˈnɔrmaːlevaɪzə] *adv*
usually

Wenn ich so schaue, geht Frauchen meistens mit mir raus.

My mum usually takes me out when I give her this look.

oft, häufig
[ɔft], [ˈhɔyfɪç] *adv*
often

Nasse Füße kann man sich in Venedig relativ oft holen.

You can get wet feet in Venice pretty often.

nie, niemals
[niː], [ˈniːmaːls] *adv*
never

You can never wait until everyone's there!

Nie kannst du warten, bis alle da sind!

Immer hast du was zu meckern.

immer
[ˈɪmɐ] *adv*
always

You're always moaning about something.

manchmal
[ˈmançmaːl] *adv*
sometimes

Manchmal ist Dolly die Einzige, die meine Gedichte versteht.

Sometimes, Dolly is the only one who understands my poems.

noch
[nɔx] *adv*
still

Bitte noch nicht abschließen, ich bin noch im Büro.

Please don't lock up yet, I'm still in the office.

noch nicht
[nɔx ˈnɪçt] *adv*
not yet

selten
[ˈzɛltən] *adv*
seldom

nun
[nuːn] *adv*
now

für immer
[fyːɐ ˈɪmɐ] *adv*
forever

der **Ort**
[ɔrt] *n*
the place

Ich wollte diesen **Ort** geheim halten, aber die Reisegruppe war mir gefolgt.

I wanted to keep this place secret, but the tourist party followed me.

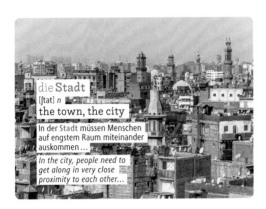

die Stadt
[ʃtat] *n*
the town, the city

In der Stadt müssen Menschen auf engstem Raum miteinander auskommen …

In the city, people need to get along in very close proximity to each other…

das Dorf
[dɔrf] *n*
the village

… im Dorf hat man mehr Platz, aber miteinander auszukommen ist deshalb nicht leichter.

…there is more space in a village, but that doesn't make getting along any easier.

der Platz
[plats] *n*
the square

Auf diesen Platz gehört ein eindrucksvolles Reiterstandbild!

What this square needs is an imposing statue of a man on horseback!

das Viertel
['fɪrtəl] *n*
the quarter

Manche nennen diesen Stadtteil das Kitschviertel.

Some people refer to this part of town as the kitsch quarter.

der Park
[park] *n*
the park

Tagsüber kann der Park wirklich schön sein.

The park can be really nice during the day.

der Friedhof
['friːthoːf] *n*
the cemetery

Auf diesem Friedhof möchte ich nicht begraben sein!

I wouldn't like to be buried in this cemetery!

nach
[naːx] *prep*
to, for

Der ICE nach Hamburg ist heute ausnahmsweise pünktlich.

The ICE train to Hamburg is running on time today, for once.

Ich glaub', dort oben kreist ein Geier.

Wo denn?

dort
[dɔʀt] *adv*
there

I think there's a vulture circling up there.

wo
[voː] *adv*
where

Where?

auf
[auf] *prep*
on (top)

Da liegt sie am liebsten: oben auf den beiden Jungs.

Her favourite place to lie is on top of the two boys.

hinter
['hɪntɐ] *prep*
behind

Hey, versteck dich nicht hinter dem Schirm!

Hey, stop hiding behind the umbrella!

die **Richtung**
['rɪçtʊŋ] *n*
the direction

Jeder entscheidet selbst, in welche Richtung er geht.

Everyone chooses their own direction.

von oben
[fɔn 'o:bən] *prep*
from above

Ein eigenartiges Licht fiel von oben herein.

A strange light shone down from above.

über
['y:bɐ] *prep*
over, above

Mein Champion hüpft über jedes Hindernis.

My Champion can hop over any obstacle.

die **Seite**
['zaɪtə] *n*
the side

Welche Seite gefällt dir besser?
Which side do you like best?

hinauf
[hɪ'nauf] *adv*
up

hinunter
[hɪ'nʊntɐ] *adv*
down

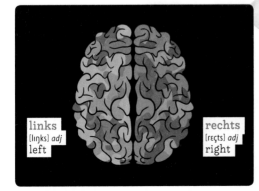

links
[lɪŋks] *adj*
left

rechts
[rɛçts] *adj*
right

vor
[fo:ɐ] *prep*
in front of

hier
[hi:ɐ] *adv*
here

oben
['o:bən] *adv*
up, on top, upstairs

unten
['ʊntən] *adv*
down (below), downstairs

in
[ɪn] *prep*
in

Ich erschrak fast zu Tode, als ich in die Kiste sah.

I got the fright of my life when I looked in the box.

um (herum)
[ʊm (hɛ'rʊm)] *prep*
around

Zum Glück wickelt sich die Schlange um den Ast und nicht um meinen Hals.

Luckily, the snake is winding itself around the branch rather than my neck.

(hin)durch
[(hɪn)'dʊrç] *adv*
through

Geht nur hindurch, und ihr werdet Augen machen!

Just go through and you'll be amazed at what you see!

unter
['ʊnte] *prep*
under

Frau Müller, was machen Sie denn da unter dem Tisch?

Ms Müller, what are you doing under the table?

neben
['ne:bən] *prep*
next to, by

Luke sitzt neben Bob, und Bob neben Warren, und Warren …

Luke is sitting next to Bob, Bob next to Warren and Warren…

hoch
[ho:x] *adj*
high

Zu diesem hohen Gipfel dort will ich heute auch noch.

I still want to make it up that high peak over there today.

draußen
['dʀausən] *adv*
outside

drinnen
['dʀɪnən] *adv*
inside

Drinnen war es auch nicht wärmer als draußen.

It was no warmer inside than outside.

niedrig, tief
['ni:drɪç], [ti:f] *adj*
low

Da stehen aber niedrige Häuser!

Those houses are really low!

Beim Stöckchenwerfen gibt es zwischen den beiden keinen Unterschied.

aus, von
[aus], [fɔn] *prep*
from

zu
[tsu:] *prep*
to, towards

an
[an] *prep*
at, on

in (hinein)
[ɪn (hi'naɪn)] *prep*
into

zwischen
['tsvɪʃən] *prep*
between

When it comes to throwing sticks, there's no difference between the two of them.

die **Farbe**
['farbə] *n*
the colour

Das indische Holi-Fest bringt
echt Farbe in unser Leben!

*The Indian Holi festival really
brings colour into our lives!*

die **Form**
[fɔrm] *n*
the shape

rund
[rʊnt] *adj*
round

die **Linie**
['liːnɪə] *n*
the line

das **Dreieck**
['draɪ|ɛk] *n*
the triangle

das **Quadrat**
[kvaˈdraːt] *n*
the square

der **Kreis**
[kraɪs] *n*
the circle

das **Rechteck**
['rɛçt|ɛk] *n*
the rectangle

weiß
[vaɪs] *adj*
white

schwarz
[ʃvarts] *adj*
black

grau
[ɡʀau] *adj*
grey

gelb
[ɡɛlp] *adj*
yellow

orange
[oˈrãːʒə] *adj*
orange

rosa
[ˈroːza] *adj*
pink

rot
[ʀoːt] *adj*
red

grün
[gʀyːn] *adj*
green

blau
[blau] *adj*
blue

violett
[vioˈlɛt] *adj*
violet

braun
[bʀaun] *adj*
brown

QUANTITIES

alle
['alə] *pron pl*
all

alles
['aləs] *pron sg*
everything

Hier bekommst du alles und kannst alle deine Wünsche erfüllen, wenn dein Kreditkartenlimit stimmt.

You can get everything here and fulfil all your wishes as long as you have the right credit card limit.

sehr
[zeːe] *adv*
very

Ich mag Tiddles wirklich sehr.
Und sie mich.

*I love Tiddles very much and
she loves me too.*

viel
[fiːl] *adj*
much

In der Koffeinbrause ist viel
zu viel Zucker drin.

*The fizzy drink contains far
too much sugar.*

viel(e)
[ˈfiːl(ə)] *pron*
many, a lot of

Für viele der Teilnehmer
war es der erste Marathon.

*For many of the racers it
was their first marathon.*

wie viel?
[ˈviː ˈfiːl] *phrase*
how much?

Wie viel verlangen Sie für
den ganzen Krempel?

*How much do you want
for the whole lot?*

etwa, ungefähr
[ˈɛtva], [ʊngəfɛːe] *adv*
about

Der Hamburger war
ungefähr so hoch.

*The hamburger was
about this high.*

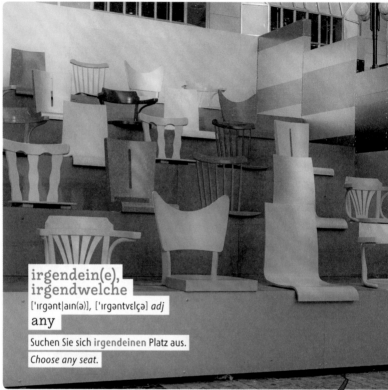

irgendein(e), irgendwelche
['ɪrgənt|aɪn(ə)], ['ɪrgəntvɛlçə] *adj*
any

Suchen Sie sich irgendeinen Platz aus.

Choose any seat.

wenig
['veːnɪç] *adj*
little, few

irgendjemand
['ɪrgənt|jeːmant] *pron*
anybody, anyone

jede(r, -s)
['jeːdə(r, -s)] *pron*
every, each

niemand
['niːmant] *pron*
nobody, no one

etwas
['ɛtvas] *pron*
something

Suchst du etwas Bestimmtes in meinen Schubladen?

Is there something particular you're looking for in my drawers?

ein bisschen
[aɪn 'bɪsçən] *adv*
a bit

… und nun noch ein bisschen Krötenschleim …

…now I just need to add a bit of frogspawn…

Ich könnte etwas mehr davon brauchen, ich bin ein Junge im Wachstum!

etwas
['ɛtvas] *pron*
a little, some

I could do with a little more than that, I'm a growing lad!

Etwas is used in German to describe an unspecified amount of a whole: Ich hätte gerne etwas Wasser (I'd like some water); Meine Schwester spricht etwas Englisch (My sister speaks a little English).

über, hinüber
['y:bɐ], ['hɪny:bɐ] *prep*
over

Gleich fließt das Wasser über den Rand.

The water is about to spill over the edge.

mehr
[me:ɐ] *adj*
more

Mehr Tattoos passen nicht drauf. Schade!

There's no room for any more tattoos. What a shame!

weniger
['ve:nɪgɐ] *adj*
less

Meine Freundin hat gesagt, etwas weniger Haare im Gesicht seien ihr lieber.

My girlfriend said she would prefer a bit less facial hair.

jemand
['je:mant] *pron*
somebody, someone

Kann mir vielleicht bitte jemand helfen?

Could somebody please give me a hand?

alle, jede(r, -s)
['alə], ['je:də(r, -s)] *pron*
everybody, everyone, each

Jeder brauchte ein eigenes Foto vom Konzert.

Everybody needed their own photo of the concert.

die **Hälfte**
['hɛlftə] *n*
the half

Welche Hälfte möchtest du?
Which half would you like?

die **Gruppe**
['grʊpə] *n*
the group

Wir müssen in der Gruppe über wirklich alles sprechen können.
We need to be able to talk about absolutely anything in the group.

genug
[gə'nuːk] *adj*
enough

Ich glaube, du hast jetzt genug Mehl, Marie!
I think you've got enough flour now, Marie!

der **Teil**
[taɪl] *n*
the part

Zumindest ist der größte Teil der Tasse noch in einem Stück.
On the plus side, the largest part of the cup is still in one piece!

das **Paar**
['paːɐ] *n*
the pair

Schau mal, ich habe ein Paar Ski im Keller gefunden.
Look, I found a pair of skis in the cellar.

nichts
[nɪçts] *pron*
nothing

Wie Sie sehen, sehen Sie nichts.
As you can see, there's nothing to see.

der **Meter**
['me:tɐ] *n*
the metre

Mein Gott, nun bist du schon einen Meter groß!

Gosh, you're already a metre tall!

Fast einen Kilometer ragt der Vulkan über dem Meer auf.

The volcano rises up almost a kilometre above the sea.

der **Kilometer**
[kilo'me:tɐ] *n*
the kilometre

die **Tonne**
['tɔnə] *n*
the ton, the tonne

Dieses Prachtexemplar wiegt fast eine Tonne.

This magnificent specimen weighs almost a ton.

das **Kilo(gramm)**
['ki:lo(gram)] *n*
the kilo(gram)

Mit einem Kilo Gold könnte ich unbeschwert Urlaub machen.

If I had a kilo of gold, I could go off on holiday without a care in the world.

der **Grad**
[gʀa:t] *n*
the degree

Unter null Grad wird Wasser zu Eis.

Water turns into ice at temperatures below zero degrees.

der **Liter**
['li:tɐ] *n*
the litre

Auf dem Oktoberfest gibt's Bier nur in Ein-Liter-Gläsern.

At the Munich beer festival, beer is only served in one-litre glasses.

der **Millimeter**
['mɪlime:tɐ] *n*
the millimetre

der **Zentimeter**
['tsɛntime:tɐ] *n*
the centimetre

das **Gramm**
[gram] *n*
the gram

das **Pfund**
[pfʊnt]] n
the pound

NUMBERS

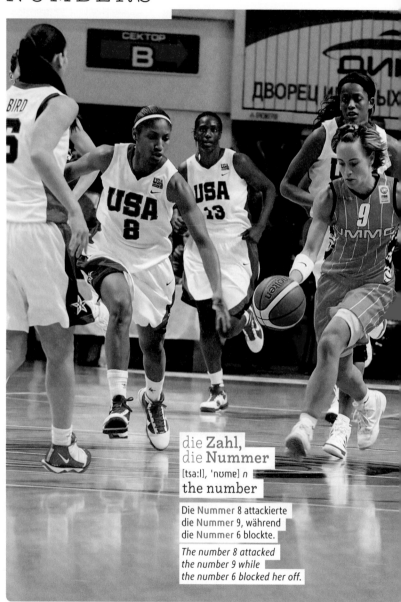

die **Zahl,**
die **Nummer**
[tsaːl], ['nʊmɐ] *n*
the number

Die Nummer 8 attackierte
die Nummer 9, während
die Nummer 6 blockte.

*The number 8 attacked
the number 9 while
the number 6 blocked her off.*

[nʊl]
zero

eins
[aɪns]
one

zwei
[tsvaɪ]
two

drei
[draɪ]
three

vier
[fiːɐ]
four

fünf
[fʏnf]
five

sechs
[zɛks]
six

sieben
['ziːbən]
seven

acht
[axt]
eight

neun
[nɔyn]
nine

zehn
[tseːn]
ten

elf
[ɛlf]
eleven

zwölf
[tsvœlf]
twelve

dreizehn
['draɪtseːn]
thirteen

vierzehn
['fɪrtseːn]
fourteen

fünfzehn
['fʏnftseːn]
fifteen

sechzehn
['zɛçtseːn]
sixteen

siebzehn
['ziːptseːn]
seventeen

achtzehn
['axtseːn] n
eighteen

neunzehn
['nɔyntseːn]
nineteen

zwanzig
['tsvantsɪç]
twenty

einund-
zwanzig
['aɪn|ʊnt-
'tsvantsɪç]
twenty-one

zweiund-
zwanzig
['tsvaɪ|ʊnt-
'tsvantsɪç]
twenty-two

dreiund-
zwanzig
['draɪ|ʊnt-
'tsvantsɪç]
twenty-three

vierund-
zwanzig
['fiːɐ|ʊnt-
'tsvantsɪç]
twenty-four

dreißig
['draɪsɪç]
thirty

vierzig
['fɪrtsɪç]
forty

fünfzig
['fʏnftsɪç]
fifty

sechzig
['zɛçtsɪç]
sixty

siebzig
['ziːptsɪç]
seventy

achtzig
['axtsɪç]
eighty

neunzig
['nɔyntsɪç]
ninety

(ein)hun-dert
['(aɪn)hʊndet]
(one) hundred

hundert-undeins
[hʊndet-ʊnd'aɪns]
(one) hundred and one

fünf-hundert
[fʏnf'hʊndet]
five hundred

1.000
(ein)tausend
['(aɪn)tauzənt]
(one) thousand

Hat der Tausendfüßler wirklich 1.000 Beinchen?
Does a millipede really have a thousand legs?

1.000.000
eine Million
[aɪnə mɪl'joːn]
one million

Eine Million Gläubige beim Gebet.
One million believers at prayer.

1.000.000.000
eine Milliarde
[aɪnə mɪ'ljardə]
one billion

Dieses Haus kostet eine Milliarde Euro.
This house costs one billion euros.

zählen
[tə 'kaʊnt] *v*
to count

Du musst bis 100 zählen ...
You have to count to 100...

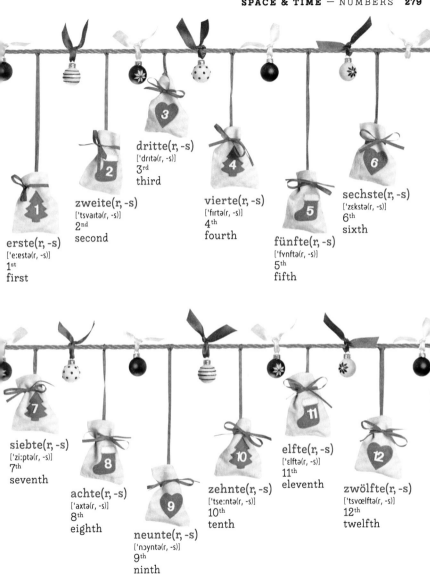

dritte(r, -s)
['drɪtə(r, -s)]
3rd
third

zweite(r, -s)
['tsvaɪtə(r, -s)]
2nd
second

vierte(r, -s)
['fɪrtə(r, -s)]
4th
fourth

sechste(r, -s)
['zɛkstə(r, -s)]
6th
sixth

erste(r, -s)
['eːəstə(r, -s)]
1st
first

fünfte(r, -s)
['fʏnftə(r, -s)]
5th
fifth

siebte(r, -s)
['ziːptə(r, -s)]
7th
seventh

achte(r, -s)
['axtə(r, -s)]
8th
eighth

neunte(r, -s)
['nɔyntə(r, -s)]
9th
ninth

zehnte(r, -s)
['tseːntə(r, -s)]
10th
tenth

elfte(r, -s)
['ɛlftə(r, -s)]
11th
eleventh

zwölfte(r, -s)
['tsvœlftə(r, -s)]
12th
twelfth

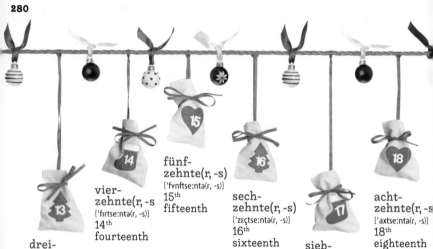

**drei-
zehnte(r, -s)**
['draɪtseːntə(r, -s)]
13th
thirteenth

**vier-
zehnte(r, -s**
['fɪrtseːntə(r, -s)]
14th
fourteenth

**fünf-
zehnte(r, -s)**
['fʏnftseːntə(r, -s)]
15th
fifteenth

**sech-
zehnte(r, -s)**
['zɛçtseːntə(r, -s)]
16th
sixteenth

**sieb-
zehnte(r, -s)**
['ziːptseːntə(r, -s)]
17th
seventeenth

**acht-
zehnte(r, -s**
['axtseːntə(r, -s)]
18th
eighteenth

**neun-
zehnte(r, -s)**
['nɔyntseːntə(r, -s)]
19th
nine-
teenth

**zwanzigs-
te(r, -s)**
['tsvantsɪçstə(r, -s)]
20th
twentieth

**einund-
zwanzigs-
te(r, -s**
['aɪnʊnt-
'tsvantsɪçstə(r, -s)]
21st
twenty-
first

**zweiund-
zwanzigs-
te(r, -s)**
['tsvaɪʊnt-
'tsvantsɪçstə(r, -s)]
22nd
twenty-
second

**dreiund-
zwanzigs-
te(r, -s)**
['draɪʊnt-
'tsvantsɪçstə(r, -s)]
23rd
twenty-
third

**vierund-
zwanzigs-
te(r, -s)**
['fiːʀeʊnt-
'tsvantsɪçstə(r, -s)]
24th
twenty-
fourth

dreißigste(r, -s)
['draɪsɪçstə(r, -s)]
30th
thirtieth

vierzigste(r, -s)
['fɪrtsɪçstə(r, -s)]
40th
fortieth

fünfzigste(r, -s)
['fʏnftsɪçstə(r, -s)]
50th
fiftieth

sechzigste(r, -s)
['zɛçtsɪçstə(r, -s)]
60th
sixtieth

siebzigste(r, -s)
['ziːptsɪçstə(r, -s)]
70th
seventieth

achtzigste(r, -s)
['axtsɪçstə(r, -s)]
80th
eightieth

neunzigste(r, -s)
['nɔʏntsɪçstə(r, -s)]
90th
ninetieth

hundertste(r, -s)
['hundetstə(r, -s)]
100th
hundredth

ENGLISH

PHOTO CREDITS

shutterstock (3), gettyimages; 137 shutterstock (6); 138 shutterstock (5), diego cervo – Fotolia; 139 shutterstock (4), Fotalia; 140 shutterstock (4); 141 shutterstock (5); 142 Shutterstock; 143 shutterstock (7), Fotalia; 144 shutterstock; 145 shutterstock (4), Fotalia; 146 shutterstock (2); 147 shutterstock (5); 148 shutterstock (4); 149 shutterstock (3), Gina Sanders – Fotolia, Jean-Pierre – Fotolia, gettyimages; 150 shutterstock (2), gettyimages, Fotalia; 151 shutterstock (2), gettyimages; 152 shutterstock (3); 153 shutterstock (6), gettyimages; 154 shutterstock; 155 shutterstock (6), fotogestoeber – Fotolia, gettyimages/Stockbyte; 156 shutterstock (4), helix – Fotolia; 157 shutterstock (3), Günter Menzl – Fotolia, gettyimages/2007 Thinkstock Images; 158 shutterstock (2), pizuttipics – Fotolia, Digital Vision.; 159 shutterstock (5); 160 shutterstock (3), Peter Atkins – Fotolia; 161 shutterstock (5); 162 shutterstock; 163 shutterstock (6), Werner Heiber – Fotolia; 164 shutterstock (3), Angela – Fotolia; 165 shutterstock (5), Jiri Miklo – Fotolia, yamix – Fotolia; 166 shutterstock (6), kab-vision – Fotolia; 167 shutterstock (4); 168 shutterstock (4); 169 shutterstock (6), gettyimages; 170 shutterstock (5); 171 shutterstock (5), gettyimages; 172 shutterstock (4), IrisArt – Fotolia, liveostockimages – Fotolia, Fotalia; 173 shutterstock (7), Erwin Wodicka; 174 shutterstock; 175 shutterstock (5), Pixelbliss – Fotolia; 176 shutterstock (4), emmi – Fotolia; 177 shutterstock (5); 178 shutterstock (5), Kadmy – Fotolia; 179 shutterstock (2), gettyimages (2); 180 shutterstock (4), Tom Bayer – Fotolia, gettyimages; 181 shutterstock (3); 182 shutterstock; 183 shutterstock (6); 184 shutterstock (3), shoot4u – Fotolia; 185 shutterstock (5); 186 shutterstock (4); 187 shutterstock (6); 188 shutterstock (5); 189 shutterstock (3); 190 shutterstock; 191 shutterstock (3), Mimi Potter – Fotolia, areafoto – Fotolia; 192 shutterstock (5); 193 shutterstock (5), fotandy – Fotolia; 194 shutterstock (5); 195 shutterstock (4); 196 shutterstock; 197 shutterstock (3), gettyimages, gandolf – Fotolia; 198 shutterstock (2), devizm – Fotolia, Freefly – Fotolia, Galina Barskaya – Fotolia, Alexander Rochau – Fotolia; 199 shutterstock (4), Dudarev Mikhail – Fotolia, gettyimages, Kirill Zdorov – Fotolia, carmeta – Fotolia; 200 shutterstock (6); 201 shutterstock (3), Lovrencg – Fotolia, PeopleImages.com – #5028ddc66a178; 202 shutterstock (5); 203 shutterstock (4), pics – Fotolia; 204 shutterstock; 206 shutterstock; 207 shutterstock (7), Tatjana Balzer – Fotolia; 208 shutterstock (2), gettyimages/2006 Jupiterimages; 209 shutterstock (5); 210 shutterstock (5), 2003 Thinkstock LLC, TOM BAYER; 211 shutterstock (3), Günter Menzl – Fotolia; 212 shutterstock; 214 shutterstock; 215 shutterstock (4), Fotalia; 216 shutterstock; 217 shutterstock (3), Victimy – Fotolia, Frank-Peter Funke – Fotolia; 218 shutterstock (4), Christian Schwier – Fotolia, DOC RABE Media – Fotolia; 219 shutterstock (4), gettyimages/Ryan McVay; 220 shutterstock (6), Claudia Nagel – Fotolia; 221 shutterstock (4); 222 shutterstock (4); 223 shutterstock (6); 224 shutterstock (2); 225 shutterstock (5); 226 shutterstock; 227 shutterstock (5), Nadine Haase – Fotolia, gandolf – Fotolia; 228 shutterstock (6); 229 shutterstock (4), akiebler – Fotolia; 230 shutterstock; 231 shutterstock (8); 232 shutterstock (6); 233 shutterstock (5); 234 shutterstock (4), Günter Menzl – Fotolia; 235 shutterstock (3); 236 shutterstock (2), gettyimages; 237 shutterstock (6); 238 shutterstock (5), gettyimages/Michael Blann, PANORAMO.de – Fotolia; 239 shutterstock (3), Daniel Strauch – Fotolia; 240 shutterstock; 241 shutterstock (7); 242 shutterstock; 244 shutterstock; 245 shutterstock (12); 246 shutterstock (6), gettyimages/2007 Thinkstock Images; 247 shutterstock (2), Fotolia, Kzenon – Fotolia; 248 shutterstock (4); 249 shutterstock (4); 250 shutterstock; 251 shutterstock (4), Alexander Rochau – Fotolia; 252 shutterstock (7); 253 shutterstock (2), Jürgen Fälchle – Fotolia; 254 shutterstock; 255 shutterstock (7), gettyimages/Thomas Northcut; 256 shutterstock (4), chesterF – Fotolia, Ansebach – Fotolia; 257 shutterstock (5); 258 shutterstock (6), Himmelssturm – Fotolia, Fotolia; 259 shutterstock (4); 260 shutterstock; 261 shutterstock (5), ErnstPieber – Fotolia; 262 shutterstock (5); 263 shutterstock (6); 264 shutterstock (3), Michael Siegmund – Fotolia, gettyimages; 265 shutterstock (3), Netzer Johannes – Fotolia, steffenw – Fotolia; 266 shutterstock; 267 shutterstock (6); 268 shutterstock (4), Paul Orr – Fotolia; 269 shutterstock (3); 270 shutterstock; 271 shutterstock (5); 272 shutterstock (4); 273 shutterstock (5), gettyimages, Fotolia; 274 shutterstock (4), gettyimages/Dennis Maloney; 275 shutterstock (7); 276 shutterstock; 277 shutterstock (25); 278 shutterstock (14); 279 shutterstock (2); 280 shutterstock (2); 281 shutterstock (8); 282 gettyimages.